~ S. Ben Qayin ~

'The Collected Writings'

Copyright

Copyright S. Ben Qayin. All rights reserved. No part of this publication may be reproduced, distributed or transmitted in any form or by any means, without the prior written permission of the author, except for brief quotations in critical reviews and other noncommercial use.
First Edition: 2020

Disclaimer

Personal success depends on work ethic, so results will vary. Consider all information adult knowledge and not legal or medical advice. Use this at your own risk. Do not violate local, national, or international laws. If any problems occur, contact a licensed psychologist or doctor immediately. S. Ben Qayin is not responsible for consequences of actions. This book is for readers of age 18 or older.

Credits

Author: *S. Ben Qayin*
Foreword: *Jon Vermillion*
Artwork: *Von Kurt*

Contents

Acknowledgments

Foreword

Introduction

1. The Cyber Vampire; *'Feeding Within The Consensual Reality Matrix'*

2. The Rites Of Wrath; *'Vengeance Is Mine'*

3. The Science Of Magic; *'All Is One'*

4. The Arte Of Blood; *'For The Blood Is The Life'*

5. Dead…But Dreaming; *'The Arte Of Necromancy, And The Calling Of The Fallen'*

6. The Crawling Chaos Of Infinite Form; *'Nyarlathotep'*

7. The Sonic Structure Of Incantations; *'Vibration Is The Key'*

Final Word

About The Author

Acknowledgements

Firstly, I would like to thank the Universe for bestowing upon me the opportunity to be in a position to share my thoughts with the world. I am honored and grateful...I also thank M., V., L., A., and B. who my heart forever resides within, I am always with you, and you with me. I thank L.A., through you I was transformed into a stronger, wiser and more awakened individual... *'You will look for me in the eyes of many, but will never find me'*...I wish you peace on your journey. I wish to thank Gary Dassing of *'Mentallo And The Fixer'* who has been a close and dear friend for many years, I couldn't have made it this far without you Brother. I thank W.V. Highlander *(David Moore)* and Paula Moore, who have shown me that there are still true and good people in the world, and that they are self-sacrificing for what is right, I consider you both a Brother and Sister in my magical tribe. I wish to thank Ian Mciver, a true and honest soul who has more talent than he even knows, thank you for all the late night talks out on the back porch. Special thanks go to Jon Vermillion for composing the *'Foreword'*, your insights on magic are valued and much needed in the world...

Thank you all...

Et Facti Deo,
~ S. Ben Qayin

Foreword

The allure of Sorcery comes from the mystical world and often entices those who see the mundane world of illusions. For centuries, Magick and Sorcery have been a driving force within spirituality, even invading the very practices within the church and other dogmatic monasteries. Magick, is but a science and this science permeates every aspect of someone's life, whether they are aware of it or not.

It takes a special Soul to climb out of the mundane and into the mystical world of Magick and Occultism. The Occult, or to be Occulted, means hidden. In many regards, unknowing minds who are not imitated into the inner mysteries feel the hidden nature is that of secrecy. The Occult sciences are not so much a mystery, or are they held secret, and the fact they are occulted from the mundane only means that one has to have to eyes to see the hidden meanings, symbols, and energy behind the physical senses which humans becomes so immersed in. These truths are always shown, but not everyone sees them.

Sorcery and Magick is a lifestyle. Some choose to wear this title proudly as a crown while others do it unconsciously, being unaware of the true nature of what is manifesting in their life and how. It is through the conscious awareness of Magick that gives power back into the hands of the once lost and gives a place within the cosmos to the soul which has felt ripped away from any true Spiritual Connection.

In recent years, we see such physical sciences such as Quantum Physics starting to touch on these fundamental occult truths. It has taken this long for science to finally catch up to what Occultists, Seers, and Sorcerers have known for aeons and they know this by the experience of direct communion. There was never any real need for "science" to prove this mystical world because those who know, KNOW. This is what makes a true practitioner of the magical arte. Luckily, because these modalities such as Quantum Physics, Quantum Mechanics, Particle Physics, and String Theory, we are seeing the concepts of Magic and Metaphysics be proven as the fabric of consciousness itself.

Everything within the spiritual world has a physical reflection. Mainstream science has become a means to disprove "God" and rip away a lot of the mystical reality behind nonphysical experiences. Over time, their "proofs" (or so they call them) have taken the magic of life and knit picked it under a microscope. Science was once the practice of proving the existence of these realities rather than taking them from the mystical world of creations true process.

"I want to know how God created this world. I am not interested in this or that phenomenon, in the spectrum of this or that element. I want to know his thoughts; the rest are details."
- Albert Einstein -

Thoughts are things and thoughts are the foundation to every aspect of magic. Whether people want to call the source or not source of creation "God", Void, the universe, or whatever title fits their paradigm, this energy invades and works through all things both physical and nonphysical. It is through this and the void aspects of creation that all things are birthed, and all things return. This happens by the mere consciousness of thought itself.

When working magic, many like to polarize the tool. From Black to White, Chaos to Ceremonial, it is all based on the same basic science and principle tools. It is how one uses it that changes its true polarity into that of a positive or negative nature.

Because magic is a tool that is your birth right, it is there for your own making and control. It is free will that drives the very current of this choice.

Black magic is the polarized aspects of the neutral scope of the craft. It is through the side of Black Magic that one truly learns to manipulate the universal forces to their own will. All Magic in essence can be looked at as Black Magic. Black is the color of mystery and the color black absorbs and contains all colors of the light spectrum. This is very important to take into consideration when thinking about Black Magic. Black is the magnetic force which draws things to yourself or others. If black contains all colors, and white reflects all colors, why would you not want to absorb all the color and information within the spectrum of totality, rather than reflecting everything off of you. This is very important when it comes to Black Magic.

S. Ben Qayin is no stranger to the occult world and through his previous writings such as *"Volubilis Ex Choasium"*, *"Thaumiel: The Dark Divided Ones"*, *"The Book of Smokeless Fire"*, *"The Black Book Of Azathoth"*, *"Harab Serapel; Ravens of the Burning God"* and *"The Book of Smokeless Fire II: Into the Crucible"*, he has shown his wide understanding of many occult truths that go unmentioned. Through his immersion into his craft he has strongly stamped his place within the spheres of influence of this world. Through the use of Chaos magic, the universe itself is created with the mere thought and intent of the magician. All these manifestations being created directly form the creational void itself. S. Ben Qayin eloquently displays spirits and non-localized intelligences such as Jinn, in a direct and concise manner, which gives the reader, researcher, or practitioner a very vivid understanding of arcane concepts.

To have such a volume produced by a mind that is no stranger to the darker concepts of magic (and the nature of Vampirism, Chaos Magic, Ritual, and Esoteric thoughts) is a great tool for a practitioner both novice or advanced to get view points on many occult subjects. Not only does it give a look through the eyes of the sorcerer, but it also will empower you to take upon the reigns yourself and gain the power that is rightfully yours.

It is through these "new" thoughts and correlations with the up and coming sciences of the world that the fabric of this world will change. It won't change from its shape or mold, but rather the fabric be utilized and made conscious. It is through the minds of new thinkers and those who think outside of the box that new arenas of Magic and realities are built. Only through this, can we truly change the world and bring back the truth and foundation of Magic as a whole.

S. Ben Qayin is one of the few that bring this type of thought to the world of Magic. Bridging both ideals of mystical magical ideologies into the perceived truths found with in quantum realities being proven today. It is only through this that a strong logical grasp upon the very nature of magic can be built. Sure, no practitioner or adept needs these sciences to prove otherwise, but these modalities of research are a valuable means to rip the attention away from the programmed mundane world into the true world of the mystical, or the true world of the nonphysical realities which are just adjacent to this one, unseen by the eyes that are too focused up on the physical illusion of mundane reality.

While reading this book, tune yourself away from the mundane physical world and connect yourself with the magical concepts held within. Only this disconnect from the Mundane will give you glimpses through the eyes of the Sorcerer.

~ Jon Vermilion

Introduction

When I began to gather all my pieces together for this volume, retrieve them from their tucked away and hidden digital alcoves, brush away the cyber dust that had collected on their virtual surfaces, I began to see how much powerful material laid before me. Re-reading each piece brought me back in memory and emotion to the time of composition, made me reminisce of different periods of my life. Some were filled of energy and excitement, written when I was so full of inspiration and joy. Others, brought me back to very dark times, their words echoing pain and desolation. Like musicians, whose music is a reflection of their trials and tribulations through life, their joys and revelations, so too do authors bleed into their creations. Each book released, mirrors that of the authors frame of mind and condition of heart. This release has the rare quality of representing not one period of my life, but many, spanning years. It is a mosaic of broken memories…

The path I have traveled over the years has been a hard one. I have traversed great gaping pitfalls and crossed vast expanses, found the hidden holy grails…and lost brothers along the way. Oftentimes the journey has been very lonesome, spending my nights in my study researching ancient grimoires for the keys that unlock their forbidden mysteries. Much goes into magic, it is not *(ironically)*, magically bestowed upon one. Countless hours of study and practice go into the *'Arte Magical'* that need be done to understand it in its entirety. Lost histories and obscure magicians must become known, archaic traditions and shadowed ceremonies understood. Though for me, understanding the workings of magic was much more than studying the past, it was also about embracing the cutting-edge philosophies of the present and expanding subject of quantum mechanics and philosophy. Knowledge is not free, and I have paid for it with my time. The subject matter of the works presented, span centuries of occult tradition and technique. They encompass a wide spectrum of discussion, from the importance of blood in magic, zombies and the undead to the science and mechanics behind what makes magic work.

It is my hope that this volume falls into the hands of those who will truly appreciate it. That it inspires and pushes forward the seeking magician to create and expand their knowledge of the Universe. Take this gnosis and put it to use well, it is yours to transmute through the magical alchemical process and make your own. Wield it in your Personal Reality Grid, and push it into the Consensual Reality Matrix for all to observe…

Et Facti Deo,
~ S. Ben Qayin

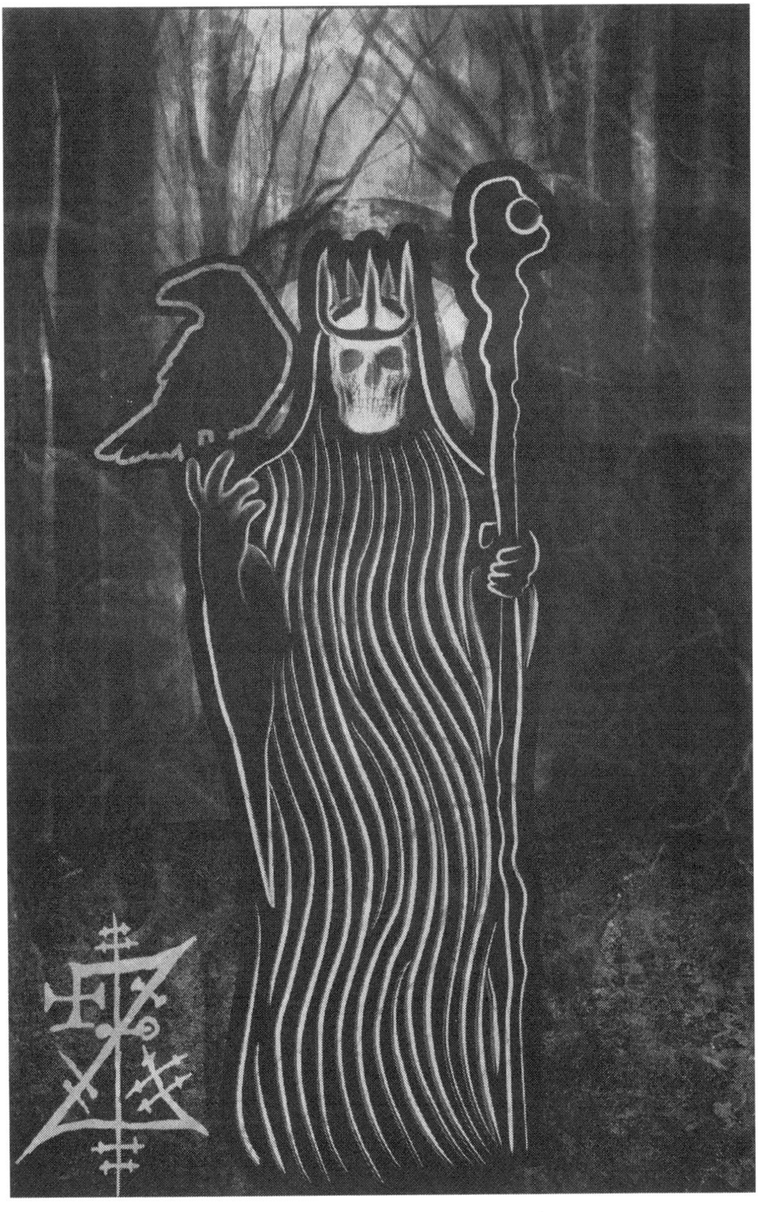

The Cyber Vampire; *'Feeding Within The Consensual Reality Matrix'*

"Will you walk into my parlour?" said the Spider to the Fly,
'Tis the prettiest little parlour that ever you did spy;
The way into my parlour is up a winding stair,
And I've a many curious things to shew when you are there."
"Oh no, no, said the little Fly, to ask me is in vain,
For who goes up your winding stair can ne'er come down again." ~ "The Spider and the Fly"
-Mary Howitt, 1829

When one begins to ponder the subject of the *'Vampire'*, generally classic images of the being instantly emerge that have long enamored and horrified the populace since time immemorial. Like other entities I have written of *(The Djinn, The Old Ones)*, the *'Vampire'*, be it in human form or not, has always been entwined with humanities shadow, for the Vampire is both within the shadow…and the shadow itself. The vampire is humanities dark reflection, concealing forbidden desires of power, lust and death that lie hidden just beneath the porcelain mask of normalcy and domestication. It is the embodiment of unrestrained freedom and life which embraces one's true will and desire, submitting to total base instinct without constraint. The Vampire is primal indulgence.

The idea of an entity that roams free in the night and drains its victims of sustenance, thus life, to in turn nourish itself, is both alluring and disturbing. It appeals to one's inner nature; to be free of one's shackles and inhibitions that constrict the soul of life itself. Yet, this is a forbidden independence that goes against the traditional laws of both man and God alike. The vampire is branded the outsider, the loner, the one who walks with death and shadows…for the vampire is a wanderer of the night and keeper of its silent secrets.

It is both this bright freedom and dark curse the vampire offers. It is a freedom that the soul needs to thrive and feel alive, though is only found outside the rigid walls and rules of accepted civilized thought. And thus, the conflict within is born. Does one give in to their screaming desires and needs, or stay a slave to the sleeping daytime world ?

The path of the Vampire is a dark and often perilous one. And, though danger surrounds, humanity is compelled to return to the being,

"The Spider turned him round about, and went into his den, For well he knew the silly Fly would soon come back again: So he wove a subtle web, in a little corner sly, And set his table ready, to dine upon the Fly."
~ *"Ibid"*

As a moth to the flame, humanity is drawn to death. Perhaps it is this same brand of curiosity that is said to have killed the cat. Humanity cannot escape this attraction, for it is ingrained within the deepest parts of man's soul and psyche. And yet, as strong as the pull of death on mortality is, the obsession to defy it seems to eclipse. There are many compelling tales throughout time of pacts with the Devil, springs of eternal life and sacred holy cups that promise such grandeur as immortality. And perhaps, there is truth to these ancient tales, as the world is a far more mysterious place than what is advertised by the common corporate masses. Though such incredible cures to death may have been achievable in their time, many have searched for a more readily available solution to the inconvenient, inevitability, of death.

Though most humans see death as final, death truly does not exist. On a quantum level all matter is composed of pure energy which cannot be destroyed or cease to be,

> *"Energy cannot be created or destroyed, but it can be transferred or transformed from one form to another (including transformation into or from mass, as matter). The total amount of energy in a closed system never changes."* ~ The Law Of Conservation Of Energy

Therefore, death is only a transformation or transference from one form to another.

However as stated, there are those who seek vampiric eternal life, youth and even supernatural abilities. A vampire is generally considered a being that absorbs an essence *(be it blood, energy, or else)* from another being either with its consent or not, depending on the morality and ethics of the vampire. There are many different kinds of vampire, though generally there are two main categories that one relates to; Sanguinarian Vampire and Psychic or Energy Vampire.

The sanguinarian vampire consumes blood from either humans or animals to fulfill a deep seeded need for energy or sustenance.

> *"For the life of the flesh is in the blood..."*
> ~ Leviticus 17:11

Yet, the energy vampire uses various techniques to obtain pure energy from the human energy field. Generally, both types of vampire utilize willing *'donors'* to obtain that which they desire. It is required they feed off of humans or animals for the energy they seek. Nevertheless, there is a more efficient way to obtain pure energy that does not depend on living creatures to be donors. The information provided here is twofold, as it gives the sorcerer access to advanced vampiric technology, while bringing the vampire into a new age of enlightenment.

> *"We are whirling through endless space, at an inconceivable speed, all around everything is spinning, everything is moving…everywhere there is energy. There must be some way of availing ourselves of this energy more directly…"*
> ~ Nikola Tesla

The above quote in its speculation could not be more correct, there is indeed a better way to *'avail ourselves to this energy more directly'*. One must tap into the pure energy of reality itself…

> *"Since time is distance in space, time is memory on the structure of space. Without memory, there is no time. Without time, there is no memory. It then follows that the energy that we perceive as the material world must be information, or energy on the structure of space."* ~ *Nassim Haramein*

> *"Concerning matter, we have been all wrong. What we have called matter is energy, whose vibration has been so lowered as to be perceptible to the senses. There is no matter."*
> ~ Albert Einstein

> *"Today a young man on acid realized that all matter is merely energy condensed to a slow vibration, that we are all one consciousness experiencing itself subjectively, there is no such thing as death, life is only a dream, and we are the imagination of ourselves. Here's Tom with the weather."*
> ~ Bill Hicks

These quotes echo the same sentiment; that at its most base composition/structure, all of existence is nothing but pure energy. This energy can be vampiricly moved from one place to another within the closed system of the Consensual Reality Matrix. All one needs is the ability to *'see'* the truth of reality, and *'accept'* into their belief system that truth to accomplish this end. That is much easier said than done, as that is the ultimate goal of the practice of magic/reality manipulation for all sorcerers. Breaking away from the dogma of illusion that surrounds is harder to get over than ingrained religious dogma, as it is the foundation upon which that later dogma was built upon. Illusions upon illusions...Breaking the structured conditioning.

> *"Dream delivers us to dream, and there is no end to illusion. Life is like a train of moods like a string of beads, and, as we pass through them, they prove to be many-colored lenses which paint the world their own hue..."*
> ~ Ralph Waldo Emerson

However, once one overcomes this hurdle, one is free. There are no more boundaries or walls to smash through. No more limits or laws. No more consensual logic. Though ironically, that is what truly terrifies so many. Once there is not the safety net of a logical structured reality to fall back upon, then one is left to freefall in a limitless solipstic solitude. Therefore, not only must one acknowledge that reality is not as it is represented to the senses, but also that we are ultimately alone in a world of our own creation.

God is alone…

Neither of these two revelations are very comforting to those so conditioned, and they may pull back from the truth. Many who fear this truth imbed themselves within religion as they find safety among the many who also seek the security of ignorance; they verify each other's reality and so cling tightly together. It is the base reason why if their religion and faith is questioned that they defend it so vehemently. They don't want to *'see'*…

> *"I'm waiting for the night to fall*
> *I know that it will save us all*
> *When everything's dark*
> *Keeps us from the stark reality…*
>
> *It's easier here just to forget fear*
> *And when I squinted*
> *The world seemed rose-tinted*
> *And angels appeared to descend*
>
> *To my surprise*
> *With half-closed eyes*
> *Things looked even better*
> *Than when they were open…"*
> ~ Depeche Mode

The Sorcerer is the center of their universe *(their Personal Reality Grid)*. All exists because they exist. Whatever the sorcerer allows to exist within their personal reality grid, exists. However, magic is where the sorcerer takes their reality and pushes it *(using Intent)* into the shared Consensual Reality Matrix *(the reality we all agree on and interact in)* through ritual, causing changes to occur that all can experience. The more energy that is pushed into magical rites, the more the Consensual Reality Matrix is changed to the will of the sorcerer. Therefore, it follows that it would be beneficial for the sorcerer to have access to vampiric occult technology that allows them to draw in this needed energy to empower their rites to the fullest.

> *"Every single one of us goes through life depending on and bound by our individual knowledge and awareness. And we call it reality. However, both knowledge and awareness are equivocal. One's reality might be another's illusion. We all live inside our own fantasies."*
> ~ Unknown

So how do we tap into this well of energy that surrounds us and creates/forms our reality; both consensual and personal ?

> *"If you want to find the secrets of the universe, think in terms of energy, frequency and vibration."*
> ~ Nikola Tesla

At its base structure, magic is composed of energy, consciousness and Intent. In fact, everything we do, be it magic or not, begins with energy, consciousness and Intent. Energy and consciousness create our reality, and Intent is the driving force behind all further thought or action. We create our reality *(the personal grid of the sorcerer),* based on what we allow ourselves to incorporate into that reality. Therefore, if reality is just a wave of energy possibilities that becomes structured to conform with our individual expectations, then it follows that if we believe we can tap into that pure energy field of all of creation, that we are already a part of and connected to, then we can.

It has been scientifically proven that we can change the structure of matter *(energy)* by focusing our Intent. This has been done with water and ice, and logically follows that all other matter is just as affected. We control our reality.
There are people who can levitate, who haven't eaten in decades, who can move objects with their thoughts. These people understand that the reality they exist in is created by their own self-imposed restrictions and have removed them.

> *"Do not try and bend the spoon, that's impossible. Instead, only try to realize the truth...there is no spoon. Then you will see it is not the spoon that bends, it is only yourself."*
> ~ The Matrix

A perfect example of creating our own reality is shown in the creation of egregores and how they come into existence. But first we must look at what *'Magic'* is. What I consider to be *'Magic'*, is nothing other than science. What else can it be ? The definition of *'Science'* is:

> *"the intellectual and practical activity encompassing the systematic study of the structure and behavior of the physical and natural world through observation and experiment"*
> ~ Oxford Dictionary

Is that definition not what the study and practice of *'Magic'* is ? Magicians study the structure of the universe and what it is composed of in its totality, in order to use advanced scientific/occult techniques in experiment, gaining experience through observation of result. One does not generally think of Magic as being a system of advanced scientific techniques, but that is exactly what it is when broken down and examined *(as I did in my works, "The*

Book of Smokeless Fire" & "The Black Book Of Azathoth"). The only true way to do that is to study all the different forms magic takes and make comparisons based on technique and result. It is a course of study I am grateful to know has no end.

As sorcerers are utilizing scientific techniques and philosophies to gain insight into the occult world, on occasion scientists too, utilize occult techniques to understand the mind, reality and existence. Science is beginning to expand its understanding and acceptance of occult principals. This is where the example of the egregore becomes relevant.

In 1972 a group of nine scientists from Ontario Canada decided to do a study on Thought Forms, and if they could create a consciousness, they could interact with by giving it a name and detailed history. After several weeks of trying to make contact with the created entity or thought form *'Philip'*, they began to get results. When asked, the created entity would recite its life and history with the exact same detail as the scientists assigned it. It responded to questions by rapping upon the table the scientists gathered around in their sessions.

In essence this occult entity or thought form was created in a lab for the scientific purpose of proving a shared fictional reality, can become a shared factual reality with enough Intent put behind its creation. Or that one's Personal Reality Grid does indeed overlap the Consensual Reality Matrix when enough energy is utilized. The implications of this experiment are vast, spanning the question of consciousness and where it originates from, to reality and the ability to mold it to our expectations.

> *"Everything you can imagine is real"*
>
> ~ Pablo Picasso

Science and magic cannot be separated or divided.

> *"Everything we consider real is made of things that cannot be considered real"*
>
> ~ Niels Bohr

Our reality, is what we make of it. Through our consciousness and Intent, we are gods of our lives and destinies.

> *"Nothing is an absolute reality; all is permitted"*
>
> ~ Bartol

Therefore, now that we have an understanding of the basis of reality, energy, magic and how entities are created, we can move forward with the vampiric applications the sorcerer can put into practice within their personal reality grid by combining these topics of discussion, and creating an egregore for the purpose of vampiricly drawing in and harnessing this energy that is the reality we are immersed in; the Consensual Reality Matrix. This energy is then utilized within the personal grid/reality of the sorcerer, to obtain desired results.

On a side note; of course one can interface with the Consensual Reality Matrix directly, but I wished to share information about the creation of egregores, energy transference and the basis of reality, so combined the subjects as a whole, as all are very complimentary and flow into one another.

Thought Forms or Egregores are quite powerful, as they stem from the mind of the sorcerer. As Athena was sprung from the mind of Zeus, so too does the sorcerer give birth to entities through their thoughts. Phil Hine states,

> *"The term egregore is derived from a Greek word meaning "to be aware of" or "to watch over". An egregore is commonly understood to be a magical entity purposefully created by a group or order as an encapsulation of the group's collective aspirations and ideals."*

As this is very true, I personally find creating an egregore for a specific task or goal that pertains directly to myself, far more beneficial. I view egregores as familiars that come and go, existing until I no longer need them, when their purpose has been fulfilled. Though the egregore can be created purposefully or not. Many times such Intent and emotion is put into a specific ideal or goal, that one is created as a sort of side effect. The sorcerer not even being aware of its creation or existence. It is very important for the sorcerer to be aware of their thoughts, as universes are created and destroyed with them.

The Vampiric Sorcerer has entered a new age, one of occult sciences that offer advanced techniques of energy transference and consumption. Reality is Energy, Consciousness and Intent. Which of these principals came to 'be' first cannot be known. Time is an illusion and that illusion is circular in nature. The Chicken produced the egg from which it hatched.

> *"I have realized that the past and future are real illusions, that they exist in the present, which is what there is and all there is."*
>
> ~ Alan W. Watts

With this knowledge all is possible. Tap into the base structure of realities veins and drink deep, fill yourself with the strength and gnosis of immortality that lies at your fingertips…*all you must do is believe.*

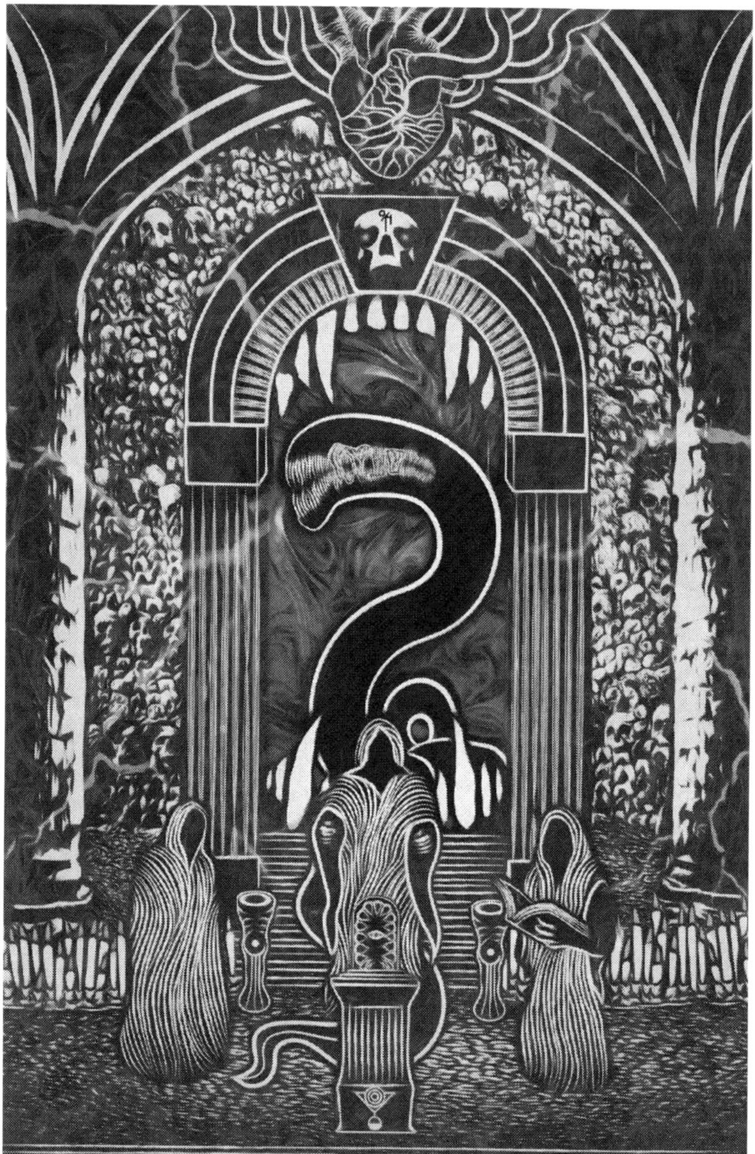

The Rites Of Wrath; *'Vengence Is Mine'*

"If your hate could be turned into electricity, it would light up the whole world"
~ Nicola Tesla

𝓗atred; a force of primal, raw, potent and powerful energy…a force born of deep personal hurt. It is an emotion that commands immediate response and conjures wild images of pain and death. This feeling has no room for anyone else but the one experiencing the possession of such a force, and the one who is on the receiving end of the fatal attention. When one is *'enraged'* , they are intently focused on destroying whatever it is that has caused the *'rage'*. They are not *'thinking clearly'* and thus conventional laws and rules no longer apply. When one is enraged they are desperate, they will do whatever it takes to satisfy the starving need for revenge which gnaws incessantly away at any remnant of reason which lies in its destructive path. They will do whatever it takes to have the chance of making their prey feel the horrible pain they themselves are enduring, to return the hurt that has been so unjustly dealt them, poured over the soul as hot tar adhering to the flesh…burning. Hatred is as a Demon which possesses swiftly as the wind, entirely consuming the mind, heart and soul in an instantaneous moment of unbearable and unbelievable exploding pain. And as quickly as it is received, the need to push this tearing misery back is nearly unstoppable, for one is consumed with the idea of brutally returning the raw anguish they are experiencing back to the source from which it fiercely and unmercilessly sprang...

The need to return the immeasurable pain, the undeniable need for revenge, is the very essence of what wrathful magic is born from. Revenge is as old as man, and man has forged many ways to harness the hatred that has engulfed his senses, through the occult magic of energy direction. When one begins to think of the methods of wrathful magic, sympathetic magic becomes prominent quickly. I have written much on the subject of sympathetic magic, its dynamics, what makes it work and the science of quantum physics behind it, so choose not to repeat what may be found within my other writings. That being said, it also cannot be entirely left out of the present work due to its core role, and so will examine it when applicable.

Wrathful magic is different than baneful magic. Baneful magic is worked against any who is so chosen by the magician. As an example; A close companion of the magician is wronged by someone and asks the magician to perform an act of bane against them. The magician can perform this task and have success. However, wrathful magic is more personal, it is the act of returning pain that has been forced upon the magician directly by another. Though one can see the similarities and connections between the two, one may also see the differences. Depending on one's upbringing and core beliefs, wrathful magic can be seen as *'Black Magic'* or taboo, going against the *'natural flow'* or order of things meant to be. In Wiccan circles this is the case, and it is believed that if a magician performs such acts, that the bane will return to the sender three-fold. This can be seen as a form of basic Karma, where if a person performs an *'evil'* act upon another, that evil returns to them in some form, plaguing their existence.

These thoughts of Karma, are said to have come from an ancient Indian religious movement known as *'Shramana'*, which later inspired such religions as Buddhism and Hinduism. This reasoning can also be seen in a parallel theme stemming from Judeo/Christian views where 'God' says unto his people that vengeance belongs to him alone.

"Dearly beloved, avenge not yourselves, but rather give place unto wrath: for it is written, Vengeance is mine; I will repay, saith the Lord."
~ Romans 12:19

And again reiterated in Deuteronomy 32:35,

"To me belongeth vengeance and recompence; their foot shall slide in due time: for the day of their calamity is at hand, and the things that shall come upon them make haste."

This way of thinking has even spilt over and been ingrained into social systems where the common phrase, *'Don't take the law into your own hands'* comes to mind and promotes helplessness. It promotes the idea of letting someone or something *'higher'* than yourself control you and your actions, it promotes complacency. Complacency is exactly what the LHP movement struggles to be free of. I don't believe in the system of Karma, I've seen too much to believe in such tales of equality. Anyone with common sense, that can truly *'see'* the world around them, knows not to believe in the mystical equality system that automatically *'rights all wrongs'* done in the world. If this were true, the world would be a much better, kinder and intelligent place.

Karma's basic bottom line is based on the idea to *'let it go'*; someone or something else will take care of it for you.

Because of these weak principals, taking the matter into your own hands is now seen as taboo in many *'civilized'* cultures, coming full circle to reinforcing the forbiddances of wrathful magic, or magic in general, as magic is self-empowering, rather than subservient. This can be seen as Order restraining Chaos.

Magic is said to not be *'Good'* or *'Bad'*, but magic. It is the one working the magic and their Intent, which weaves magic into benevolence or bane. Though since all realities and perspectives of individuals differ from one another, and there are so many definitions of *'Evil'*, (as Thomas Karlsson so well points out in *"Qabalah, Qliphoth And Goetic Magic"*) that good and bad no longer have a separate meaning. They are simply and complexly, two sides of the same coin. Essentially this would mean anything goes when one is *'Enlightened'* enough to come to this conclusion.

However this seems to not be the case when it comes to the Church of Satan, for even in this swirling vortex of realities and abstract moral codes, there have been laws or guidelines laid down, a foundation of Order within the Chaos. We see this reflected in Anton *LaVey's "The Eleven Satanic Rules Of The Earth"*, which speak of not stealing, hurting children or killing. Yet the COS speaks of embracing indulgence. Truly the laws themselves are in direct opposition to the enlightenment obtained which implies there are no restrictions. This is a direct contradiction.

> *"Do What Thou Wilt Shall Be The Whole Of The Law"* ~
> *Aleister Crowley*

As for Crowley, he also believed in embracing ones inner wants and needs, and taught that all are on their own path, and in order to obtain enlightenment of who they truly were/are as individuals, limitations, laws and restrictions must be ignored and broken for this to be experienced, to become, *'Wholly Oneself'*. Ultimately in my personal view, what *is*, or *is not* evil comes down to the individual and their Intent. No act is *'Evil'* unless one feels in their heart it is so and proceeds all the same. This is *'Evil'* because the act damages and weakens the black magician and their reality. A good example of this would be addiction; repeatedly performing an act that one knows is damaging to the self and possibly others, but does so anyway, to fulfill a selfish need they fight to control. My point here is, no one can define what is truly *'Evil'*, as no one sees from the same perspective. Yes, general guidelines can be agreed upon, but it truly comes down to the individual's personal core beliefs and moral values when confronted with a situation which requires their action and choice, when no one is there to watch or judge them. So, is it right or wrong to perform wrathful magic ? Well, that all depends on the individual and what they allow to exist in their *'Personal Reality Grid'*.

Hatred is an emotion I am very familiar with, it is my *'Dark Passenger'*. Hatred has been my most powerful ally, and most deadly foe. Hatred is the double-edged sword which I respectfully grasp within my hands; if not wielded correctly, it will bring me to my knees. It is deadly and unforgiving. I have learned through painful lessons that hatred has no master, for hatred is born of True Chaos, and will not be contained. Hatred has taken up a permanent residence within me, when once it only came to visit, I believe this is because I have come to *'see'* the world around me and the potential it has, but will never reach due to mass ignorance, selfishness shortsightedness, of the human populace. On my crooked path in this life, I have had many come against me, unjustly cause me pain, and try to outright physically kill me. I have experienced much hatred for the individuals that inflicted these woes upon me and have performed rites that worked in wrathful ways against them. However, now I find my hatred has not only moved in, but also grown to encompass the populace on a mass, general scale. I have written,

> *"They say that between madness and genius there lies a fine line that is easily crossed, a path that can be traversed without notice, where one eventually looks up, and finds that they are indeed on the other side of the looking glass, though have no recollection of having made the trip"*
> ~ *"Volubilis Ex Chaosium"*

Upon reflection, I have come to the solitary conclusion that it is *'Potential'* that makes the genius *'Mad'*. For me, as said, it is the potential of what humanity could be, of what it could learn and create…but will never obtain due to short sightedness and pure greed; the greed to control, to put all in *'Perfect Order'*. Having the ability to *'See'* the potential, and not having the power to cultivate it and bring about a mass change is what drives me/one *'Mad'*. My hatred of people is difficult to explain, I don't hate them, they are beautiful, they have so much they could do with the compassion and intelligence they have access to, but they refuse to have the courage and awareness to draw from these fountains of true enlightenment. And for this, I have come to hate them, they have driven me *'Mad'*, in both senses of the word.

To dig and examine deeper; what causes the ignorance of the mundane is what should truly be hated. The cause or root of the problem must be attacked and destroyed to cure the world and peace be finally known. What causes the ignorance is Order…all seeing, all controlling, Order. To combat this ever-imposing Order, pure raw Chaos must be unleashed to balance it. And so I have released *"The Book Of Smokeless Fire"*; an Infernal work of bane...against Order itself. The weight of releasing such a book of hate upon the world is much, and I hope that in the end it will have served its purpose and be seen as a terrible but needed instrument for liberation. For it fights the restraining forces of Order with all there is to attack it with, to bring it down and be free of its shackles so that freedom and creativity may again reign. To obtain the paradise we know should exist; we must first walk through the desolate Shadows in the Valley of Death. After a fire has consumed a land and left it charred, new untainted, unrestrained growth again springs forth from the Earth. We need a fire...

And though *"The Book of Smokeless Fire"* is an act of wrath against the main forces of Order in general, it attacks the *'Whole'* by attacking the many that it is composed of. These attacks will be carried out by Black Magicians seeking dark justice. The book acts as both a personal weapon, and one that also strikes on a mass level. It will be through personal pain, that the world is transformed.

There are many methods of wrathful magic, however utilizing techniques of sympathetic magic, as mentioned, seems to be the most preferred because of its effectiveness. Wrathful magic is personal, and therefore requires personalization to be effective. Though this is a bit like saying one must hold their breath when underwater, it is obvious and instinctual. When one is enraged, the rite performed can be nothing but personal, the rite becomes as natural as breathing itself. The direction of this baneful energy alone, is often enough to cause the desired end *(though often undirected, causing random chaos)*. This has been referred to as *'The Evil Eye'*. Menasseh ben Israel writes,

> *"The angry glance of a man's eye calls into being an 'evil angel' who speedily takes vengeance on the cause of his wrath."*
> ~ The Sefer Hasidim

This is an interesting statement, in that it suggests that the act of *'Looking'* and *'Directing Bane'* alone, is enough to call forth *(and even create)* spiritual agents to act out the will of the seer. It is a ritual of seeing alone and can even be viewed as the act of creating a malevolent egregore to carry out the wrathful will of the operator.

However, if one wishes to be more *'Exact'* in their inflicting bane, ritual structure is employed. This act of ritually releasing hatred has taken many forms, from Vodoun hex dolls, to inciting spirits to attack ones victim. Though, regardless of the form of the rite, the energy/emotion behind the act is the key to its success. Generally magic is performed by acquiring the needed personal energy, building it up to a climax, and then releasing it in a directed manner. With wrathful magic, the required personal energy to perform the rite is already overflowing and must be directed with Intent. The sooner a rite of wrathful magic is performed after the offense inflicted, the better; as the energy utilized is fresh, genuine, raw and powerful. This is not a magic that you want to try to recall your feeling of hatred for, but instead let forcibly break free from the fresh open wound it has gashed within. Wrathful magic is a living, breathing, directed force.

When one begins to concentrate on the subject of wrathful magic, generally sympathetic magic is counted as a major vehicle for such rites to work through. Nevertheless, there have been many documented cases where spirits have been employed by the will of a magician to attack his/her foes. There is a case that is quite famous and that I find interesting, that documents a sinister spirit's continued attacks on a family unsuspecting. This occurred in 1761 at The Lamb Inn, in Bristol. There was a very powerful *'Chief of Familiars'* by the name of *'MALCHI'* employed by a black magician/witch to torment the family of Mr. Giles. The entire family was tortured with physical injury and death. Only when another Sorceress was employed, did the horrendous attacks yield. This is one of the best documented cases of spiritual wrathful magic to date. Of course, when discussing this subject, Aleister Crowley comes to mind as well. Crowley and Samuel Mathers *(as most know)* had a falling out *(like so many of Crowley's relationships)* and began a spiritual war with one another. When I say spiritual war, I mean to say, they sent vicious spiritual entities to each other for the sole purpose of the others destruction. Mathers initiated the assaults, by evoking Typhon-Set who it appears, killed Crowley's pack of bloodhounds and then went on to spread sickness to all his servants, making them very ill. Crowley in return, evoked Beelzebub and his forty-nine servitors to plague Mathers. And, in the end, Crowley seems to have been the victor, as Mathers died in 1918 of mysterious, unknown causes.

Interestingly in connection with Crowley, Jack Parsons also performed a wrathful rite. It was performed against Ron L. Hubbard of Dianetics/Scientology, when Hubbard left Parsons and their joint boat dealing business. Hubbard escaped Parsons on a boat with the destination being a port in Florida. In retaliation, Parsons summoned Bartzabel; Demon of Mars; controller of Storms, and indeed a storm did rise, causing the sails to be ripped from Hubbard's boat and forcing the vessel back to port where Hubbard was detained by the Coast Guard. Crowley never liked Hubbard, believed him a con-artist, and foretold of the betrayal to Parsons. And, in the end, Hubbard was forced by court order to repay all debt owed to Parsons...

Wrathful magic has a long and painful history, the most deadly and potent of curses have been dragged forth from the wounded hearts of individuals, to strike at their foes like vicious snakes, hell-bent on revenge. There are some very famous curses which many know of, yet do not know their origin. One such interesting curse is from the Shakespearian play *"MacBeth"*. It is said that Shakespeare may have obtained the baneful spell in the play from a true coven of Witches, and that if spoken bane would follow, encompassing the name of the play itself. The reason for this is because the Witches are said to have cursed Shakespeare himself as well as the play for all eternity. Interestingly, the play does indeed have a very dark history that has followed it when performed. And until this day, thespians shun the utterance of the dreaded name; *"MacBeth"*,

> *"Round about the cauldron go;*
> *In the poison'd entrails throw.*
> *Toad, that under cold stone*
> *Days and nights has thirty-one*
> *Swelter'd venom sleeping got,*
> *Boil thou first i' the charmed pot.*
>
> *Double, double toil and trouble;*
> *Fire burn, and cauldron bubble.*
>
> *Fillet of a fenny snake,*
> *In the cauldron boil and bake;*
> *Eye of newt and toe of frog,*
> *Wool of bat and tongue of dog,*
> *Adder's fork and blind-worm's sting,*

Lizard's leg and owlet's wing,
For a charm of powerful trouble,
Like a hell-broth boil and bubble.

Double, double toil and trouble;
Fire burn and cauldron bubble.

Scale of dragon, tooth of wolf,
Witches' mummy, maw and gulf
Of the ravin'd salt-sea shark,
Root of hemlock digg'd i' the dark,
Liver of blaspheming Jew,
Gall of goat, and slips of yew
Silver'd in the moon's eclipse,
Nose of Turk and Tartar's lips,
Finger of birth-strangled babe
Ditch-deliver'd by a drab,
Make the gruel thick and slab:
Add thereto a tiger's chaudron,
For the ingredients of our cauldron.

Double, double toil and trouble;
Fire burn and cauldron bubble.
Cool it with a baboon's blood,
Then the charm is firm and good."

~ Shakespeare, 'Macbeth', Act Four; Scene One

Another rite of wrath is the spoken Catholic curse/ritual known as Excommunication. One does not normally think of the rite as an act of wrath, even though it very much is, The Church is personally offended, and thus drives the individual out. For one devoted to Catholicism, it is the worst curse one could be branded with. The Priest personally curses the victim being excommunicated, to suffer in eternal Hell Fire,

> *"The rite is equivalent to a curse, and involves a bell, the Holy Book, and a candle. There is a sentence which the priest reads:*
>
> *We exclude him from the bosom of our Holy Mother the Church, and we judge him condemned to eternal fire with Satan and his angels and all the reprobate, so long as he will not burst the fetters of the demon, do penance and satisfy the Church.*
>
> *The priest then closes the book; rings a bell, which symbolizes a toll of death; and extinguishes the candle and throws it down to symbolize the removal of the person's soul from the sight of God."*
> ~ Guiley, 'The Encyclopedia of Witches and Witchcraft"

Wrathful magic is a magic of deep, maddening, personal pain. Those who utilize such a malefic magic feel as though their very essence is on fire, burning through their veins when wielding it…it is the only way this type of magic can be drawn upon. Using this magic is, and is not, *'Evil'*, depending upon the Magician's perspective of their reality. These rites outlined may seem harsh and destructive to some. However, when the day comes that they are shaking with rage and hurt from an unjust affliction dealt them, they may *'see'* differently, and remember this weapon called *'wrath'* that rests at their fingertips…

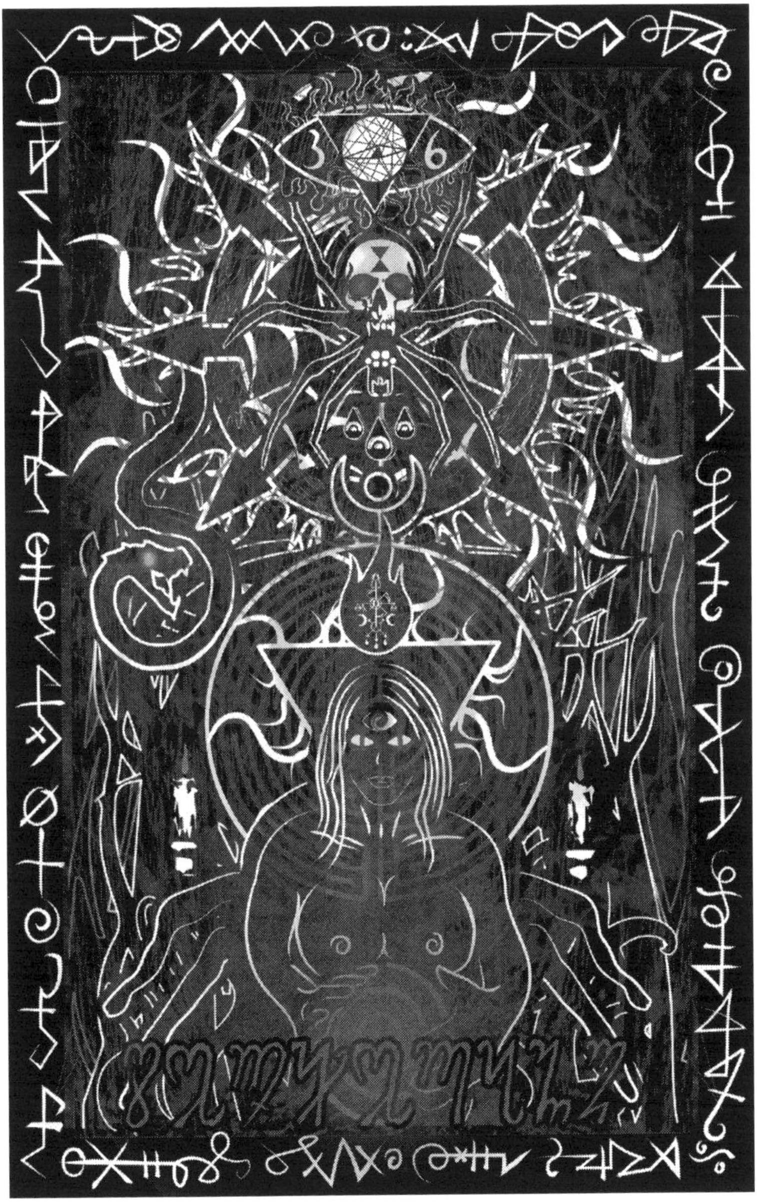

The 13 Pillars Of Wrath

*H*ere I will present a rite which I have personally found effective when wanting to return the pain inflicted on me by my foes. I have decided to include a personal sympathetic magic rite, rather than one originating from *"The Book of Smokeless Fire"* simply because the book is very dangerous and must be read and understood before using. I recommend to those wishing to inflict ancient infernal damage onto their foes, obtain a copy.

This particular rite is designed to transfer the hate the magician feels, into an item that represents and connected to the intended victim, causing direct influence to them. Here sympathetic magic is utilized, though the scientific community will recognize this as an act applying what is known in quantum physics as entanglement.

What is needed is relatively simple, truly a magician needs nothing to perform a rite, all comes from within,

> *"We don't need anyone to teach us sorcery, because there is really nothing to learn. What we need is a teacher to convince us that there is incalculable power at our fingertips…Every warrior on the path of knowledge thinks, at one time or another, that he's learning sorcery, but all he's doing is allowing himself to be convinced of the power hidden in his being, and that he can reach it."*
> ~ Don Juan, 'The Power of Silence'

Therefore, few ritual tools are needed to perform this rite successfully. You will need something from the victim, hair, fingernail clippings etc.; something that not only belongs to them, but that *'is'* them. As well, you will need a piece of paper, a black hilted dagger, something to write with, a coffin nail or three, and your blood.

Begin with casting a double circle upon the ground roughly six feet in diameter for the inner circle, with the outside circle three inches further out. Once done, place 13 'X' marks around the circle somewhat evenly *(chalk works best for this rite)* so the middle of the 'X' is in between the two concentric circles. Create the circle in white or black and the 'X's', in red if possible. When drawing this circle imagine a red-hot flame bursting forth from your hands, let your hatred burn through you. When making the 'X's'; cast them as if you were violently slashing at your enemy with a blade. Place 13 black candles upon the 'X's' in the double circle. These candles should be anointed, charged and carved with the appropriate tinctures, energies and sigils beforehand to empower the rite even more so, as the flame activates the malefic energies within each of the 13 candles. The circle is now purely a vehicle to be used for the wielding of wrath.

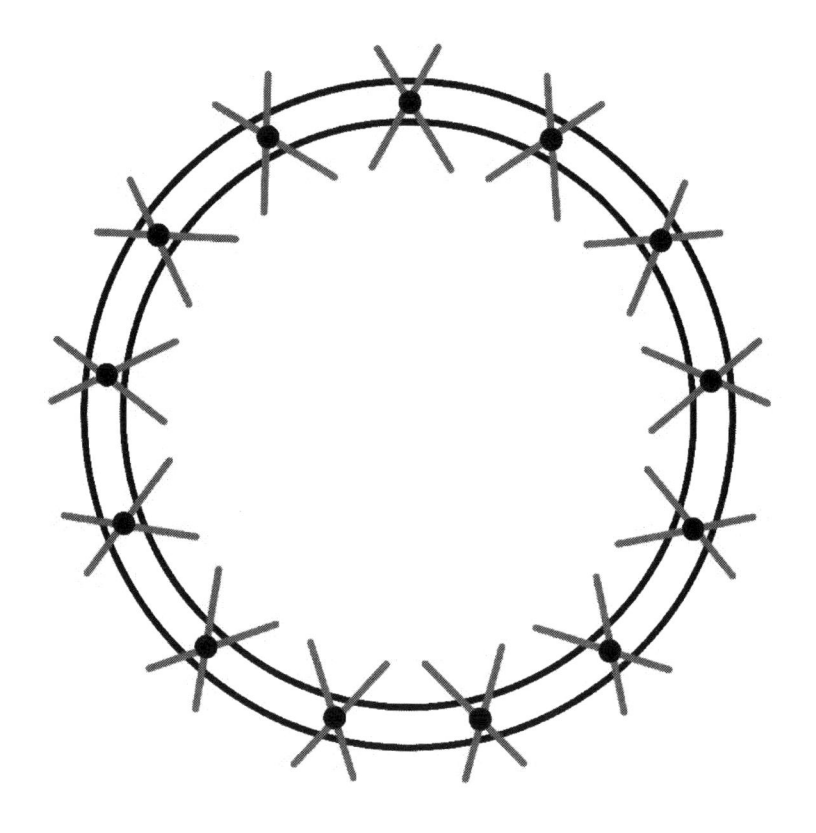

When you begin the rite, start by standing in the circle facing north, and with your dagger firmly in your left hand, trace a pentagram in the air in front of you. Moving counterclockwise, repeat the same gesture for the remaining three cardinal points until you again face north. Evoke the powers of Darkness and Death. Call out to them to surround you and feed off the energy being released. Call for them to hear your words and aid you in the deliverance of your wrath *(the Magician may use Spirits from their own personal system here)*. Call forth to any surrounding Demons who may hear your call, invite them to gather round and aid you in whatever way they will.

These entities will help infuse the rite with the proper energy needed. Call,

"Eternal Darkness of the Abysmal Void,

Great Shadow of eternal being,

I call you forth…

Gather round this Infernal circle of destruction,

Fuel the fire of vengeance that burns fiercely within my being,

Deliver my envenomed Intent…

Holy Death that ever stalks,

Come close, see my pain that lies before you,

Call up the sacred Dead of earthly decay,

The Nightshades of timeless vision that creep in deathly silence,

Encircle me with their presence and power,

Spirits of Darkness and Death,

Empower this rite of hatred,

Intensify it so it may not fail…

Guide my hate swiftly as an arrow pierced through the heart,

Bring down mine enemy…"

After you have made your calls and evocations, sit within the circle and meditate/relive the memory of the offense cast onto you by your victim. Once filled with pure hatred, write the victim's name in three groups of three upon the paper already procured. Once done, use your blood to 'X' out each group of three, leaving a total of three bloody 'X's' upon the paper when done. When creating the 'X's' over the names, again focus your anger into the act; imagine your victim feeling your intense rage as you cross them out of existence. The blood and pain represent personal anguish, commitment to the bane performed and brings forth the required energy to help complete the work. It makes manifest in the material world, what is only experienced on an emotional/spiritual level. Focusing this level of hatred within such a charged circle, along with the bloodletting, provides enough energy to be massed and released into the Consensual Reality Matrix, causing the desired end to occur within the reality, and/or personal Grid of the Magician.

Once the 'X's' have been cast over the names, place your victim's hair, nail clippings, etc. in the center of the paper. Then, take the piece of paper into your hands and crush it into a tight ball with all of your might, release all of your anger, all of your hatred…all of your rage. Beat your fists upon the ground and let your hatred flow through your hands into the paper, scream out your protest to their existence. Take the coffin nail and drive it through the paper as driving a spear through your enemy, let this be your last and final fatal blow. If you have three coffin nails, all the better. Coffin nails provide the link with Death energy, directed by hatred. More than likely, you will have bruises from this come the following day. When the coffin nails have all been driven, call out to the Lord of Darkness to bless your wrathful act, and to oversee that justice is done. Leave the paper within the circle overnight, the following night bury it at the base of an oak tree, dead or alive. Oak is the wood of the crossroads. At this point, the rite is finished, go about your business and think not of those who came against you, for you have put into play strong malefic energies that will indeed run their course…

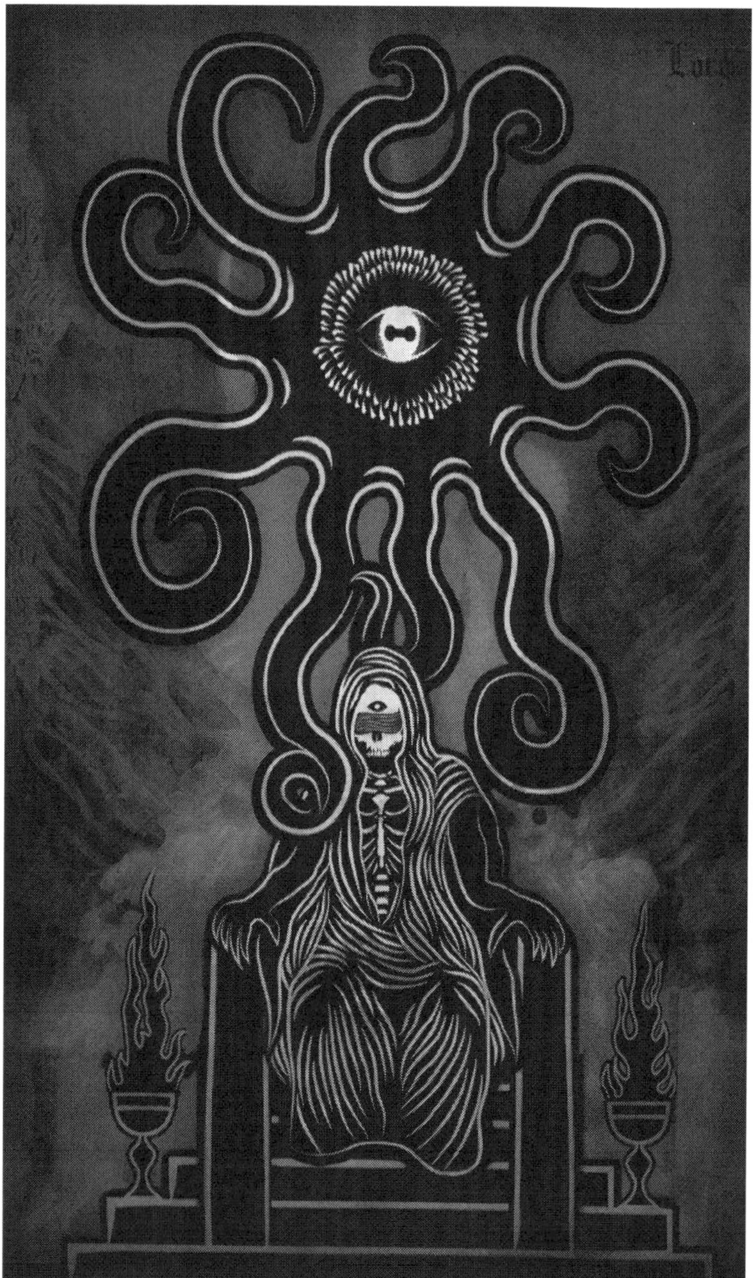

The Science Of Magic; *'All Is One'*

"It is for the philosophic student to trace the train of thought which underlies the magician's practice; to draw out the few simple threads of which the tangled skein is composed; to disengage the abstract principles from their concrete applications; in short, to discern the spurious science behind the bastard art."

~ Frazer, *"The Golden Bough"*

For aeons sympathetic magic has been utilized to work countless rites in witchcraft and sorcery throughout the world, and has proved to be one of the most effective and influential means to obtain a magical desired end, encompassing everything from love to death, in cultural practices universally. These practices have been viewed in large by the majority of the scientific community as primitive and quite useless.

It is only now that advanced science is producing the same effects that magic has been producing all the while. The same exact results and principals are being pondered and put to use that have been in use for ages. This is a turning point in man's history, a revelation to be had, illumination to be basked in, for man has so much potential, if only he could embrace the possibilities of *'Otherness'*.

The concept of Sympathetic Magic has been around since there has been magic, which is essentially since there has been man. However, Sir James George Frazer first categorized this system of magic into two distinct groups so that they may be more readily understood and scientifically analyzed. The first of the groups he titled *'Similarity'*, and the second group *'Contact or Contagion'*, he writes,

> *"If we analyze the principles of thought on which magic is based, they will probably be found to resolve themselves into two: first, that like produces like, or that an effect resembles its cause; and, second, that <u>things which have once been in contact with each other continue to act on each other at a distance after the physical contact has been severed.</u> The former principle may be called the Law of Similarity, the latter <u>the Law of Contact or Contagion</u>. From the first of these principles, namely the Law of Similarity, the magician infers that he can produce any effect he desires merely by imitating it: from the second <u>he infers that whatever he does to a material object will affect equally the person with whom the object was once in contact, whether it formed part of his body or not."</u>*
> ~ The Golden Bough

Frazer did not believe in the system of magic, in fact found it ridiculous,

> *"<u>If my analysis of the magician's logic is correct, its two great principles turn out to be merely two different misapplications of the association of ideas</u>. Homoeopathic magic is founded on the association of ideas by similarity: contagious magic is founded on the association of ideas by contiguity. Homoeopathic magic commits the mistake of assuming that things which resemble each other are the same: contagious magic commits the mistake of assuming that things which have once been in contact with each other are always in contact. But in practice the two branches are often combined; or, to be more exact, while homoeopathic or imitative magic may be practiced by itself, contagious magic will generally be found to involve an application of the homoeopathic or imitative principle. Thus generally*

stated the two things may be a little difficult to grasp, but they will readily become intelligible when they are illustrated by particular examples. Both trains of thought are in fact extremely simple and elementary. It could hardly be otherwise, since they are familiar in the concrete, though certainly not in the abstract, to the crude intelligence not only of the savage, but of ignorant and dull-witted people everywhere. Both branches of magic, the homoeopathic and the contagious, may conveniently be comprehended under the general name of Sympathetic Magic, since both assume that things act on each other at a distance through a secret sympathy, the impulse being transmitted from one to the other by means of what we may conceive as a kind of invisible ether, not unlike that which is postulated by modern science for a precisely similar purpose, namely, to explain how things can physically affect each other through a space which appears to be empty."

Ironically the definition of *'Entanglement'* used in quantum physics states exactly what Frazer claims as idiotic and is believed by magicians that are of a,

"..crude intelligence not only of the savage, but of ignorant and dull-witted...".

The definition of *'Quantum Entanglement'* is thus,

"<u>Quantum entanglement is a physical resource, like energy, associated with the peculiar nonclassical correlations that are possible between separated quantum systems.</u> Entanglement can be measured, transformed, and purified. A pair of quantum systems in an entangled state can be used as a quantum information channel to perform computational and cryptographic tasks that are impossible for classical systems. The general study of the information-

processing capabilities of quantum systems is the subject of quantum information theory."

~ Stanford Encyclopedia of Philosophy

Sympathetic magic works, it has always worked. Ironically, science is finally catching up with magic, and not vice versa as was always predicted by the scientific community. And so now we enter an age where science is ever moving closer to what we have termed as *'Magic'* all those many moons ago.

Teleportation is very closely related to *'Entanglement'*. It is a process created in a scientific lab where a particle is teleported across the room from point: A, to point: B. H.P. Lovecraft speaks of teleportation,

"...What made the students shake their heads was his sober theory that a man might - given mathematical knowledge admittedly beyond all likelihood of human acquirement - step deliberately from the earth to any other celestial body which might lie at one of an infinity of specific points in the cosmic pattern.

Such a step, he said, would require only two stages; first, a passage out of the three-dimensional sphere we know, and second, a passage back to the three-dimensional sphere at another point, perhaps one of infinite remoteness. That this could be accomplished without loss of life was in many cases conceivable. Any being from any part of three-dimensional space could probably survive in the fourth dimension; and its survival of the second stage would depend upon what alien part of three-dimensional space it might select for its re-entry. Denizens of some planets might be able to live on certain others - even planets belonging to other galaxies, or to similar dimensional phases of other space-time continua - though of course there must be vast numbers of mutually uninhabitable even though mathematically juxtaposed bodies or zones of space.

<u>It was also possible that the inhabitants of a given dimensional realm could survive entry to many unknown and incomprehensible realms of additional or indefinitely multiplied dimensions - be they within or outside the given space-time continuum</u> - and that the converse would be likewise true. This was a matter for speculation, though one could be fairly certain that the type of mutation involved in a passage from any given dimensional plane to the next higher one would not be destructive of biological integrity as we understand it...<u>Professor Upham especially liked his demonstration of the kinship of higher mathematics to certain phases of magical lore transmitted down the ages from an ineffable antiquity - human or pre-human - whose knowledge of the cosmos and its laws was greater than ours.</u>"

~ H.P. Lovecraft, *"Dreams in the Witch House"*

Lovecraft has ever infused our idea of interdimensional travel with angles. Angles beyond reason, *"an angle which was acute, but behaved as if it were obtuse..."* as he describes in *"The Call Of Cthulhu"*. Angles are the key to unlocking the dimensions, the key to traveling *'In-between'* just as Keziah Mason used them to escape her prison cell in, *"The Dreams in the Witch House"*,

"...not even Cotton Mather could explain the curves and angles smeared on the grey stone walls with some red, sticky fluid."... "She had told Judge Hathorne of lines and curves that could be made to point out directions leading through the walls of space to other spaces beyond, and had

> *implied that such lines and curves were frequently used at certain midnight meetings in the dark valley of the white stone beyond Meadow Hill and on the unpeopled island in the river"*

One could only draw the natural conclusion that within angles, there is power. And within the *'Correct'* angles, doorways between realms can, will, and have opened. If the correct angles are utilized in conjunction with the correct vocal vibrations, such as in the evocation of Yog~Sothoth given in *"Volubilis Ex Chaosium"*, doors to other dimensions reveal themselves, and are unlocked for travel, both to and from the *'Other Point'*. At this juncture between dimensions often lie guardians or guides that one must either master or follow, such as Choronzon, Papa Legba, Nyarlathotep, etc., depending on which system of magic is being utilized.

Though angles may be the *'Key'* to opening portals to the *'In-between'*, embracing the *'Otherness'* does not come without its wear on the human psyche, and is often associated with obsession,

> *"As time wore along, his absorption in the irregular wall and ceiling of his room increased; for he began to read into the odd angles a mathematical significance..."*

> *"For some time, apparently, the curious angles of Gilman's room had been having a strange, almost hypnotic effect on him; and as the bleak winter advanced he had found himself staring more and more intently at the corner where the down-slanting ceiling met the inward-slanting wall."*
> ~ H.P. Lovecraft, *"The Dreams In The Witch House"*

This is a reoccurring theme when using Lovecraftian based magical paradigms. In *"The Pseudonomicon"*, Phil Hine states in the disclaimer of the book,

> *"It is generally agreed by experienced magicians that working with the Cthulhu Mythos is dangerous due to the high risk of obsession, personality disintegration or infestation by parasitic shells…"*
> ~ Phil Hine

And to quote from *"Volubilis Ex Chaosium"*,

> *"It is advised that one working this system should already be familiar with ceremonial magic and its various traditions and foundations. Also be aware that this series of workings can be dangerous both physically and psychologically, the entities that are to be called forth are among the most feared in Chaos Magic, and conventional magical laws are not always applicable to, or observed by, these beings."*
> ~ S. Ben Qayin

These entities are real, they are powerful and can be very devastating to work with. They are raw primal Chaos itself, in its most basic of forms. Lovecraft as well as Macgregor Mathers both suffered greatly physically and mentally when working with the Old Ones as described in *"Volubilis Ex Chaosium"*. Pete Carroll adds his own warning as well from his online blog,

> *"Lovecraft's 'Elder Gods' have dangerous Promethean and Luciferian types of knowledge, knowledge with which we could easily destroy ourselves: - Direct power over the mind and the brain itself, power over the core processes of biology, the power of creating life and physical immortality, the understanding of the strange and secret*

geometries of the universe at both the cosmic and quantum levels, and the power to manipulate them, the powers of chaos and of creation itself."
~ Pete Carroll

Science is just now accepting and recognizing that many of the *'Old Myths'* hold great truth in being literal rather than metaphorical in nature. These *'Stories'* whether they be carved into the side of an ancient temple wall, or printed in a pulp fiction magazine, hold very real truths that can unlock our shrouded past if viewed in the right context, that of course being open mindedness. For the Universe holds more secrets than one can ever imagine or unravel. And though we have *'Scientific'* laws and systems in place that are said to govern our *'Reality'*, they are constantly being revised and replaced with new more advanced thought and practice that an older way of thinking has long embraced in its occult traditions. Breathe in new concepts, ideas and change, for that is the very essence of the Left Hand Path, for the path of Chaos has no one form...Change must always occur...

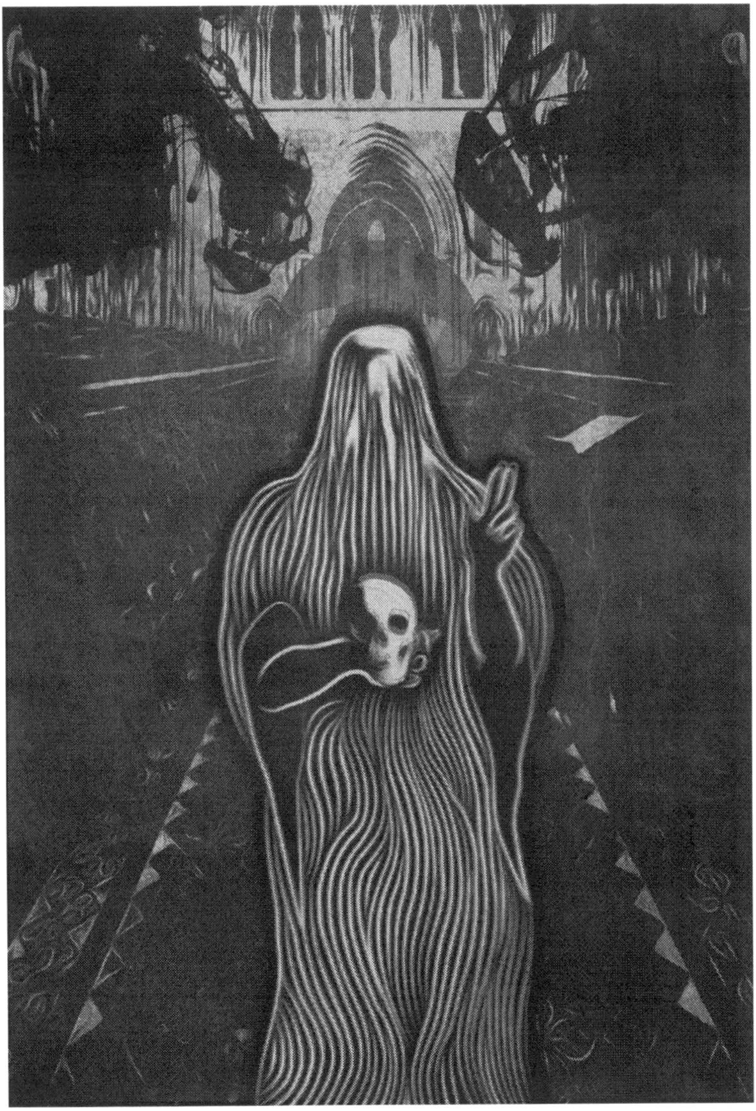

The Arte Of Blood; *'For The Blood Is The Life'*

*"Blood is an hourglass of a thousand sands…
Each grain a desert,
With the thirst of a thousand dying men…"*
~ S. Ben Qayin

Blood…glorious elixir of life, that which brings light to the darkened eyes of lone night shades, giving breath again to those who dwell in shadow light. It is the fiery essence of magic run course through your burning veins, and the strength of the consuming spirits that drink in its power, who ever wander the halls of endless mists. Blood has an energy to it that many react to; there is something inherently *'forbidden'*, or sacred that we feel when experiencing it. It is our essence, the spirit liquefied and warm…it is Alchemical, as both a material and a spiritual essence combined into one ever changing beautiful form which gives life and possess power… it is existence.

Much has been written of blood in connection with the spiritual. It has drawn our attention as a race and been woven into our sacred and holy rites throughout history, imbedded within both philosophic and theological thought, as well as in ritual praxis as central religious applications and symbology. In the Christian bible their god is quoted as saying if one drinks of it, they shall be *'Cut Off'* from heaven and salvation,

"For it is the life of all flesh; the blood of it is for the life thereof: therefore I said to the children of Israel, You shall

eat the blood of no manner of flesh: for the life of all flesh is the blood thereof: whoever eats it shall be cut off."
~ Leviticus 17:14

And yet within their very own rites of Eucharist, they drink wine which is magically/alchemically transformed into the blood of their savior, which makes for an interesting contradiction to the previous passage considering Jesus' own words,

"He who eats My flesh and drinks My blood has eternal life, and I will raise him up on the last day. For My flesh is true food, and My blood is true drink. He who eats my flesh, and drinks my blood, dwells in me, and I in him."
-John 6:54

Regardless, it is seen by Christians as something sacred that either belongs only to their god, or that can only be consumed by followers from the veins of the son of their God, Jesus Christ. Holy blood is also a reoccurring theme in the phenomena known as *'Stigmata'*, which occurs to believers of Christ who wish to feel his sacrifice and pain. Often the supernatural scene is filled with sacred blood,

"All of a sudden there was a dazzling light. It was as though the heavens were exploding and splashing forth all their glory in millions of waterfalls of colors and stars. And in the center of that bright whirlpool was a core of blinding light that flashed down from the depths of the sky with terrifying speed until suddenly it stopped, motionless and sacred, above a pointed rock in front of Francis. It was a fiery figure with wings, nailed to a cross of fire. Two flaming wings rose straight upward, two others opened out horizontally, and two more covered the figure. **And the wounds in the hands and feet and heart were blazing rays of blood.** *The sparkling features of the Being wore an*

expression of supernatural beauty and grief. It was the face of Jesus, and Jesus spoke. **Then suddenly streams of fire and blood shot from His wounds and pierced the hands and feet of Francis with nails and his heart with the stab of a lance.** *As Francis uttered a mighty shout of joy and pain, the fiery image impressed itself into his body, as into a mirrored reflection of itself, with all its love, its beauty, and its grief. And it vanished within him. Another cry pierced the air.* **Then, with nails and wounds through his body, and with his soul and spirit aflame, Francis sank down, unconscious, in his blood."**

~ From A Treasury of Catholic Reading, ed. John Chapin (Farrar, Straus & Cudahy, 1957)

Not only is blood seen and utilized as a path that leads to enlightenment, but pain as well. One sect of the Dervishes in Arabia known as the Rufai, or *'Howling Dervishes'* also use blood and pain to elevate their minds to a state of heightened spiritual awareness called *'Melboos'*. Another well known Sufi sect is the *'Swirling Dervishes'* who spin round until a trance is laid upon them and they find union with *'God'* which they view as life itself and interestingly, that they themselves are *'God'* as well. Unlike the Swirling Dervishes, the Rufai are known to inflict physical pain upon themselves in place of *'Swirling'*, to enter into *melboos* so that they may commune with *'God'*, or the self in a heightened spiritual trance state.

"...The Rufai, or Howling Dervishes who slash their bodies with knives and burn themselves with red-hot irons...In front of them was a brazier, with a glowing bed of charcoal, from which emerged the handles of knives, long iron pins, like spits, with wooden handles, and iron pokers with no handles at all. "

~ W.B. Seabrook, *"Adventures In Arabia"*, 1927

This scene is also described by Seabrook,

"Suddenly one of the Dervishes leaped to his feet, threw off his cloak, leaped again into the air, naked to the waist. The Rufai sheik leaped up at the same time, seized a long, red-hot spit by its wooden handle from the brazier, and began waving it wildly in the air...the other Dervish circled, leaping around the sheik and howling, then backed, with his head pressed sideways against the wooden pillar, with his mouth gaping open, and stood rigid, motionless. The sheik inserted the spit at an angle into his mouth, and with a solid blow of his fist drove it through the man's cheek and pinned him to the pillar."

~ W.B. Seabrook, *'Adventures In Arabia'*, 1927

I have personally experienced a very similar ritual where I rose above the pain that was inflicted and became *'One'* with the Universe. I was fortunate to be in a circle of friends who were suspension artists, and one night I was given the rare opportunity to partake in one of their sacred rites. I was pierced with two six gauge, four foot long crisscrossing spears through my back and one six gauge, two foot long spear through both cheeks with my mouth open, *(very much like the Dervish as described)* as well as two more smaller 10 gauge needles pierced through my lower lip. I now intimately relate to this particular kind of unique experience in the quest for finding oneself, or *'God'*. When in such a state, reality is suspended and in place of feeling pain, one rises above it and *'Rides'* it. The intense pain thrusts the mind and spirit into a state of excitement where ones extra sensory mode is activated and one not only feels life around him, but *'Sees'* life around him. The energy that resonates off a person while experiencing this transcendent state is quite amazing, it's as if they are *'Cracked'* open and the energy that lies beneath their material *'Shell'* radiates out as a star burning its brightest and hottest before it goes out, as the rituals usually don't last more than an hour. It is something I find difficult to describe, as it is such a personal experience, and differs from one individual to another. Though, one thing that is always universally experienced among practitioners is the spiritual feeling of freedom, being alive and connected to all, in a moment frozen in time.

These are just a few examples of the use of blood and pain within different cultures and religious movements of the world. There are many, many more examples, as blood is seen as symbolic for a great multitude of religions and spiritual reasons ranging from life and death, to being purified to unclean. Of course, Pagans and Magicians also view blood as a spiritual essence, though it is seen as something more personal that does not belong to a God, but to them. It is embraced as life, but also serves as a reminder of death, being seen as magical, having unique properties that can be utilized in many different ways concerning ritual and as an agent in contacting spiritual entities. This is age old tradition still being put to use by many modern practitioners and occult orders, especially in the rapidly growing LHP movement along with the new interest in the Afro-Brazilian religious traditions, such as Quimbanda, Palo Mayombie and Voudon.

Personally, I use blood in many rituals and workings, I always have. It is something very sacred to me. In my eyes, it serves as a sign of devotion as well as sacrifice. Within my spiritual beliefs, I kneel before no God, though offer them my essence out of respect and to empower the rite. I see most entities as being equal, some have been here longer than me and have more knowledge and experience, but that does not make them superior to me, only more learned. And, as more learned, they should know this and have the same respect for me, as I do them, equally. Else, why would I commune with them as spiritual brothers ? I offer them sacrifice, not out of fear, but honor and respect. I beg no entity or God to change things in my life, I ask them to help me as a brother, who walks the same crooked path as they do, and if I can help them in turn, then I gladly do.

My first use of blood in magic was when I was in my teenage years; *(buying what I could of magic books that were to be found at the bookstore in the mall)* no system that I had found then really resonated with me, so I created my own from elements I did resonate with, from within various systems. I didn't realize at the time that I had just taken my first step on the path to becoming a Chaos Magician. I came to understand that the one dominate reoccurring magical factor in my life was the moon, I was drawn unnaturally *(or supernaturally)* to the moon. Not only that, but huge life changing events would occur on the first three nights of the waxing crescent moon, to the point that the connection could not be ignored, even by the most skeptical. Therefore, I began honoring it as a sentient being, and quickly found that my life was infused with incredible luck and magic, as if all life's doors were suddenly open, and I could walk through whichever ones I chose at my leisure with ease.

I would take a wooden box that served as my altar, that I had painted with various symbols *(some known, and others my own)* along with my ritual supplies, up to the top of a large wooded hill that overlooked the city. It was quite beautiful and I would often encounter deer and other wildlife on my journey upward. Once there I would lie out my altar and tools, light the altar candle and meditate on my current position in life, what was important and that which I desired to change. I then would cut my left arm with a clean razorblade three times, deep enough to let blood flow just a trickle *(there is always such a spiritual release that I experience when this occurs, it is no different for me now then it was for me then)* and spread a good amount of blood on a dead leaf that I had procured on the trip up the mountain. Once done, I would burn the leaf so that my essence would entwine with the energy of the night as the smoke would rise to caress the moon. At that point in the ritual I would partake of the blood myself, enjoying tasting the raw energy of life itself dance upon my tongue…As said, I had tremendous positive results with this, and still do when practiced, though the ritual has grown to encompass much more meaning and depth.

Of course, now that I am older and have experienced more than what the new age books of the mall had to offer, I work with blood in a more complex way. I have found that spiritual activity is greatly increased when blood is used in ritual. I find this because the energy that is being released by the magician acts as a beacon in the spiritual world, attracting many different curious entities. It is such a personal offering that the magician can fully immerse himself in ritual and the spiritual world, so contact with an entity is stronger and a bond formed.

Naturally, blood is also used in a lot of sigil work I undertake. I believe blood helps to bring *'Life'* to a sigil if created with it. This of course again connects the magician with the spiritual entity that is being called forth, creating a pact of sorts as it is the essence of the magician *(blood)*, conjoined with the essence of the spirit *(sigil)*. I see ritual as something very private that takes place between myself and the spirits, something that others should not see. It is a time when my earthly skin is shed, and my spiritual being can fully breathe in the night and embrace the spirits on their ground. It is something sacred and beautiful and should be respected and seen as such. When one works with blood, spirits, and the night, an amazing collage of magic is painted upon the canvas of reality, immersing the magician in a state of non-reality where the miraculous is able to be brought forth into the magician's plane of awareness. This twilight of the In-Between is where magic is performed, it is where time and space cease to exist and action occurs.

In my book, *'Volubilis Ex Chaosium'*, blood is used to draw the Old Ones close,

> *"Throughout the history of magic, blood has been used as a means to attract spirits and to be used as an energy source for them to materialize into visible appearance before the magician. Blood is used in these workings as an energy source for the Old Ones to be drawn to the Trinity Of Triangles so that interaction may occur, in whatever form it may take. Blood is the eternal energy and essence of all life. It is the most sacred and personal offering that one can make to the Gods. There are many examples of the use of blood sacrifice in 'Yog~Sothothery', and is definitely a reoccurring theme when evocation of a said entity is to be called forth. Therefore staying true to Lovecraft's visions, it has been employed in this magical system."*

I have found the spiritual interaction within V.E.C., very powerful and effective, as it deals with the very *'edge'* or outer realms of the magical Universe in experimental realms such as the *'Tunnels of Set'* also known as the *'Vaults Of Zin'*, or what may be called the *'Nagual'* (drawing from Don Juan's terminology), though it still utilizes traditional ritual elements within its structure. And, within this system, blood and pain are used, as in the *'Nyarlathotep Initiation Ceremony'*, as a way to both heighten and excite the spiritual mind of the magician to a level of awareness that is needed for communion with the Old Ones.

There are also a great many who hold the belief that ingesting blood infuses one with spiritual strength or *'energy'*, resulting in vampiric qualities including heightened senses both spiritually and physically, as well as immortality of either the physical or ethereal body. There have been many throughout history who have been known to utilize blood as an element for the rejuvenation of life. One of the most famous; Elizabeth Bathory, was known to have bathed in, and drank, the blood of over 650 young women in efforts to remain young and live forever. There are reports stating that her desired end result of youth was somewhat achieved, until she was jailed of course.

Though, through the ages a division has been made manifest between the material and the spiritual aspects of blood. There are now recognized vampires who only consume the *'Life Force'*, or *'Prana'* of a person that is carried by the blood throughout the body, rather than ingesting the blood itself, this is well known as psychic vampirism. *'The Temple Of The Vampire'* is one such religion which recognizes this praxis as a core pillar in their religious construct.

They hold the belief that they are evolved humans who drink in the personal energy of lesser humans and store it. When enough energy is collected, they enter into a ritual they call *'Communion'* where they freely release all their stored energy to the *'Undead Gods'* in return for the Undead Gods to release their Vampiric energy upon them. With each transfusion of life-force, they become less human, taking on the qualities of their ascended masters.

> *"The Vampiric Condition is, therefore, a condition of evolution actualized by the exchange of Life-force energy with Those Who Have Risen (The Undead Gods) above the restriction of a physical body."*
>
> ~ T.O.T.V., *'Revelations'*, 2006

However, within their Temple, blood drinking is looked down upon,

> *"Drinking physical blood is a socially unacceptable behavior and reveals a deep misunderstanding of our religion."*
>
> ~ T.O.T.V., *'Website'*, 2012

Although this view is not always agreed upon between Vampires and the personal beliefs they hold, and therefore the practice of blood drinking as an energy source is still utilized by many underground societies as well as in individual solitary praxis,

> *"The grand fantasy that many would be vampires have in these modern times is that the physical consumption of blood is wholly unnecessary for the vampire's maintenance of immortal existence. This is a basic fallacy stemming from the most recent resurgence in the occult movement of the 1990's…'The simple truth of the matter is that the vampire must, in conjunction with vital energy manipulation, (which begins with techniques of visualization) consume large quantities of food that contains exceedingly high amounts of life-force, prana, etc'…'Now, the truth of the matter is that human blood, being the substance of life for the most highly cognitive and evolved species on this planet, contains the most concentrated degree of life-force available."*

~ A.W. Dray, *'Nox Infernus'*, 2011

The spectrum for the uses of blood in the areas of religion and magic is vast. Another area of interest is the use of blood as a medium for divination. The specific name or names for this are *'Hematomancy'* or *'Haematomancy'*, which breaks down to, Haimat = Blood, and Manteia = Prophecy. Dririmancy is specifically divination by observing dripping blood and the patterns it creates upon whatever surface is being utilized in the ritual. One similar method of spiritual contact that can be utilized, is the use of blood in conjunction with mirrors to open gateways. This is seen in an anonymous rite that was included in Scarlet Imprint's, *"Diabolical"*. The practitioner adorns a full length mirror with demonic sigils drawn of their own blood, especially where the infernalist's face and heart will appear in the reflection. Once done, the Demon is evoked/invoked into the reflection of the magician. This is a very effective operation, as it again relates to connecting the magician to the spirit being called forth through the mirror, by the use of sigils and blood. As stated, this type of bond formed with a spiritual entity is amazingly strong and cannot be easily broken.

Blood…We instinctively know its strength, we feel its seductive rhythm pounding through the world as the drums of destiny pushing us ever forward into the *'Night of Times'*, pounding as our hearts beat within our own chests, breathing life within our flesh and making *'Alive'*, that which would not be. For it is the blood of *'God'*…of *'Self'*…of *'Being'* that courses through our veins and bestows upon us the very fragile and easily extinguished flame we call existence. Drink in its essence, feel it flow through you, for this is magic in its purest and strongest form, a magic that ever changes as the raging force of untamed Chaos itself.

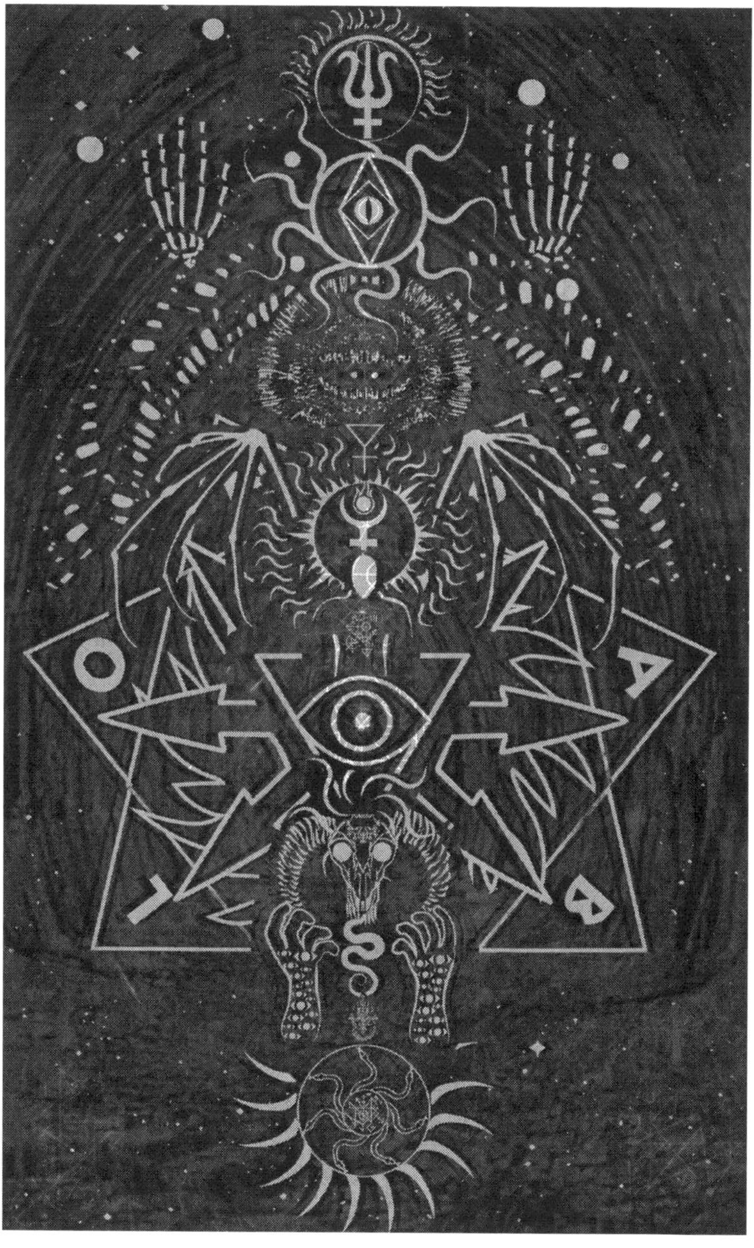

Dead...But Dreaming; *'The Arte Of Necromancy, And The Calling Of The Fallen'*

"Death, the inexorable and pitiless, is it but a release, the separation of the liberated spirit from the biologic matter? Or is death actually the final destruction, a total annihilation against the resurrection of a new life in the morning sun? Does death lead to the total darkness of the night or does it bring the vaunted light to the souls eagerly searching for the portals of eternal life?
~ Dr. Emile Laurent, *'Magica Sexualis'*, 1934

The realm of the Dead; The ethereal shadow land that lies parallel to the dense world of the living, just out of sight as a specter itself on the edge of breathing reality. It has been said that the fog like barriers that separate our worlds can be magically worn down, and communication made possible with those who have crossed over into the cold twilight of un-death, still existing, though without the beat of a heart within their chest or the feel of warm blood running course through their now barren veins. The Dead are known to forever wander between the worlds, gliding in the shadows, thin as smoke, caressing the world of the living with their cold waif like tendrils.

Magicians have long sought the council of the fallen Dead, seeking secret knowledge of lost and hidden things, of treasure and the forbidden future. Necromancy or *Nekuomanteia [Greek]: Necro- Dead, Manteia- Divination,* has been practiced for thousands of years, being traced back to Babylonian Chaldea and Egypt, though has been most commonly recorded in Greek history. The first mention of Greek Necromancy was in Homer's *"Odyssey" (700-650 B.C.E)*, where Odysseus raised the Dead through the instruction of the Witch Circe.

Very little history of this *'Arte of the Dead'* exists, so much is spread out over time and location. Of course there is ancestor worship and the honoring of ancestors recorded in many lands, though it is not held in the same category as calling the dead forth for the sole purpose of divination with the exceptions of religions such as Palo Mayombe, where it is quickly seen that ancestors *are* called forth from the Spirit World and employed for various reasons including protection of oneself and home, among many others, including divination which will be examined further on.

One of the main reasons Necromancy was practiced, was to *'lay restless ghosts'*. That is, bring to peace Spirits who for some reason could not be content to go on with their existence in the Spirit World, and remained in that of the living. The Spirits would bring attention to their trouble at hand so it may be resolved, and they may finally rest. Necromancy eventually evolved to include divination and was practiced in places called Oracles of the Dead named, *'Nekuomanteions'* that were generally located underground or within cemeteries or crypts of the deceased. These were secret gathering places that operated unseen from the condemning eyes of the masses, once Necromancy was seen as vulgar and outlawed. These Oracles were in such places that desolation knew well. They have always been in areas that Death frequents and casts His influence on, such as ancient battlefields, gallows trees, or in areas where violent death has occurred.

There have been noteworthy Magicians throughout history who have worked this forbidden *'Arte of the Dead'*, some unexpected, such as Jesus of Nazareth who rose Lazarus as well as others. Though I don't consider Jesus *(existing or not)* a true Necromancer, as he did not raise the dead for prophecy, but to show people that his father *'God'* had chosen him to deliver God's holy word *(slavery)* to them. Of course, when one conjures the images of Necromancy, the famous scene depicting John Dee and Edward Kelly speaking with a Spirit in a cemetery, while inside a magical circle, comes to mind. However, truly it was not Dee, but Paul Waring in Walton-le-Dale, near Preston in Lancashire, who performed the rite with Kelly. One of the most detailed accounts of Necromancy comes from a rather celebrated Magician, Eliphas Levi. Levi was hired by a rather mysterious woman dressed entirely in black with a black veil covering her face, who wished to call up the philosopher Magician, Apollonius of Tyan. Levi writes of his amazing experience raising the Spirit,

"...I was clothed in a white garment, very similar to the alb of our Catholic priests, but longer and wider, and I wore upon my head a crown of vervain leaves, intertwined with a golden chain. I held a new sword in one hand, and in the other the ritual. I kindled two fires with the requisite prepared substances, and began reading the evocations of the ritual in a voice at first low, but rising by degrees...the smoke spread, the flame' caused the objects upon which it fell to waver, then it went out, the smoke still floating white and slow about the marble alter; I seemed to feel a quaking of the earth, my ears tingled, my heart beat quickly. I heaped more twigs and perfumes on the chafing-dishes, and as the flame again burst up, I beheld distinctly, before the altar, the figure of a man of more than normal size, which dissolved and vanished away. I recommenced the evocations and placed myself within a circle which I had

drawn previously between the tripod and the altar. Thereupon the mirror which was behind the altar seemed to brighten in its depth, a man's form was outlined therein, which increased and seemed to approach by degrees. Three times, and with eyes closed, I invoked Apollonius. When I again looked forth there was a man in front of me, wrapped from head to foot in a species of shroud, which seemed more grey than white. He was lean, melancholy and beardless, and did not altogether correspond to my preconceived notion of Apollonius. I experienced an abnormally cold sensation, and when I endeavored to question the phantom I could not articulate a syllable. I therefore placed my hand upon the sign of the pentagram, and pointed the sword at the figure, commanding it mentally to obey and not alarm me, in virtue of the said sign. The form thereupon became vague, and suddenly disappeared. I directed it to return, and presently felt, as it were, a breath close by me; something touched my hand which was holding the sword, and the arm became immediately benumbed as far as the elbow. I divined that the sword displeased the spirit, and I therefore placed its point downwards, close by me, within the circle. The human figure reappeared immediately, but I experienced such an intense weakness in all my limbs, and a swooning sensation came so quickly over me, that I made two steps to sit down, whereupon I fell into a profound lethargy, accompanied by dreams, of which I had only a confused recollection when I came again to myself. For several subsequent days my arm remained benumbed and painful. The apparition did not speak to me, but it seemed that the questions I had designed to ask answered themselves in my mind..."

~ Eliphas Levi, *'Transcendental Magic, Its Doctrine and Ritual'*, 1896

Ironically, Apollonius practiced Necromancy himself by raising the famous Spirit of Achilles. Unlike most Necromantic rites, he did not perform a rite at all, and offered none of the traditional libations to bring forth the Spirit. Instead, he offered but a simple prayer or calling to the Ghost,

> *"O Achilles, most of mankind declare that you are dead, but I cannot agree with them, nor can Pythagoras my spiritual ancestor. If then we hold to the truth, show to us your form; for you would not profit not a little by showing yourself to my eyes, if you should be able to use them to attest to your existence."*

Traditionally there are several different methods for evoking the Dead, or holding congress with them in the Underworld. One method stems from the honoring of ancestors by way of libation of various substances. This account of practice is detailed in Homer's *"Odyssey"* where Odysseus *(as mentioned)* raises the Spirit Tiresias; a blind prophet who would reveal the future of his *(Odysseus)* journeys, who dwells in Hades. When in the Underworld, Odysseus begins his Necromantic Arte by first digging a sacrificial pit to hold the libations to be used. Once done he pours a mixture of milk and honey around the pit, followed by sweet wine and finally fresh spring water, all of which are in the end, sprinkled over with barley. When all libations have circled the sacrificial pit, a prayer is given to the Dead pledging them upon returning to the world of the living, the best sterile heifer of the heard, and 'treasures' to be burnt upon a pyre in their honor. Once this recitation has commenced, a separate and personalized prayer is offered the Spirit, in Odysseus' case, Tiresias, that promises *(again, upon his safe return)* the sacrifice of an all black ram. At last, with a bronze sword, he bleeds two black sheep of opposing sex into the prepared sacrificial pit, at which point the Dead appear and draw near to quench their thirst and obtain the strength and life energy that lies within the spilt blood. Odysseus is in need of the bronze sword to keep the Spirits at bay, keeping them clear of the blood which gives them the ability to speak and have tangibility. Odysseus proclaims to the restless Dead,

> *"With my sharp sword again unsheathed I watched over the pit of sacrificial blood, lest any of the fragile dead draw near that blood before I met Tiresias."*

Only is Tiresias allowed to partake of the blood so that intended interaction may occur. This use of a sword in Necromancy is largely reminisant of Levi's already given account, and is a recurring theme or element within this praxis. It is interesting to note that a physical sword, surly being magical, has the ability to harm a spiritual entity. This belief is also a central theme in Arabic mysticism concerning Djinn.

The use of Blood Sorcery in Necromancy is also very important. Blood is a vital power source to be used by the Dead to appear and communicate. Though there are other rites of evoking the Dead, they generally take many days to gather the needed energy for the Spirit to appear. However when blood is utilized, its energy is so strong that the Dead can easily draw from it what they require for interaction with the Magician almost immediately.

Blood Sorcery has been practiced since man began to use Magic. A true Magician naturally feels and understands that this personal substance that gives us life, is powerful without equal. It is the ultimate sacrifice when given, the ultimate energy source for Spirits of all kinds to draw from, and the Magician's personal life signature. It is the Spirit in material form, the *'Philosophers Stone'* of crimson red. I have written on this subject at length in a piece titled, *"The Arte Of Blood"* featured in *"Qliphoth"* Opus II, so I will not go on here, except to reinforce the necessity of this vital liquid in rites concerning quickly drawing forth the fallen Dead.

Another interesting example of Necromancy, resides in Lovecraft's work, *"The Case of Charles Dexter Ward"*, where Ward recites a Necromantic evocation to raise his ancestor. The rite involves Yog-Sothoth as the *'Keeper of the Crossroads'*. Whether fact or fancy, it is interesting none the less. The rite involves having the *'salts'* or ashes of the deceased and reading an evocation. The use of *'salts'* in Necromancy has been described by Borellus, a seventeenth century philosopher/alchemist,

"The essential Saltes of Animals may be so prepared and preserved, that an ingenious Man may have the whole Ark of Noah in his own Studie, and raise the fine Shape of an Animal out of its Ashes at his Pleasure; and by the lyke Method from the essential Saltes of humane Dust, a Philosopher may, without any criminal Necromancy, call up the Shape of any dead Ancestour from the Dust whereinto his Bodie has been incinerated."
~ Borellus

The evocation to raise the Dead is as follows,

"Per Adonai Eloim, Adonai Jehova, Adonai Sabaoth, Metraton On Agla Mathon, verbum pythonicum, mysterium salamandrae, conventus sylvorum, antra gnomorum, daemonia Coeli God, Almonsin, Gibor, Jehosua, Evam, Zariatnatmik, veni, veni, veni. (Said in repetition for two hours),

DIES MIES JESCHET BOENE DOESEF DOUVEMA ENITEMAUS !

Yi-nash-Yog-Sothoth-he-lgeb-fi-throdog-Yah !

Y'AI 'NG'NGAH,

YOG-SOTHOTH,

H'EE-L'GEB,

F'AI THRODOG,

UAAAH !"

And to lay the Dead to rest again, the evocation is repeated, with the omission of the last section to be replaced with,

"OGTHROD AI'F,

GEB'L—EE'H,

YOG-SOTHOTH,

'NGAH'NG AI'Y,

ZHR !"

There are other lengthier methods of calling the Dead forth, this next example is again related by Levi, though I hesitate to quote here as it is lengthy, but find it such an exact description of this specific Arte of the Dead, that I have decided to include it here for those who are in need of this information and wish to follow its example. The ceremony/ritual is accessible from a LHP point of view, as there are no Holy orations or devotions given to the

Demiurge. Where such is needed or wanted, the Magician applies patron deities as they desire. This rite is designed to focus on the Spirit being called forth, not on a Deity or the Magician himself/herself. The procedure is as follows:

"We must, in the first place, carefully collect the memorials of him (or her) whom we desire to behold, the articles he used, and on which his impressions remains; we must also prepare an apartment in which the person lived, or otherwise, one of similar kind, and place his portrait veiled in white therein, surrounded with his favorite flowers, which must be renewed daily. A fixed date must then be observed, either the birthday of the person, or that day which was most fortunate for his and our own affection, one of which we may believe that his soul, however blessed elsewhere, cannot lose the remembrance; this must be the day for the evocation and we must provide for it during the space of fourteen days. Throughout this period we must refrain from extending to anyone the same proofs of affection which we have the right to expect from the dead; we must observe strict chastity, live in retreat, and take only modest and light collation daily. Every evening at the same hour we must shut ourselves in the chamber consecrated to the memory of the lamented person, using only one small light, such as that of a funeral lamp or taper. This light should be placed behind us, the portrait should be uncovered and we should remain before it for an hour, in silence; finally, we should fumigate the apartment with a little good incense, and go out backwards. On the morning of the day fixed for the evocation, we should adorn ourselves as if for a festival, not salute anyone first, make but a single repast of bread, wine, and roots, or fruits; the cloth should be white, two covers should be laid, and one portion of the bread broken should be set aside; a little wine should also be placed in the glass of the person we design to invoke. The meal must be eaten alone in the

chamber of evocations, and in the presence of the veiled portrait; it must be all cleared away at the end, except the glass belonging to the dead person, and his portion of bread, which must be placed before the portrait. In the evening, at the hour for the regular visit, we must repair in silence to the chamber, light a fire of cypress wood, and cast incense seven times thereon, pronouncing the name of the person whom we desire to behold. The lamp must then be extinguished, and the fire permitted to die out. On this day the portrait must not be unveiled. When the flame is extinct, put more incense on the ashes, and invoke God according to the forms of the religion to which the dead person belonged, and according to the ideas which he himself possessed of God. While making this prayer we must identify ourselves with the evoked person, speak as he spoke, believe in a sense as he believed; then, after a silence of fifteen minutes, we must speak to him as if he were present, with affection and with faith, praying him to manifest to us. Renew this prayer mentally, covering the face with both hands; then call him thrice with a loud voice; tarry on our knees, the eyes closed and covered, for some minutes; then call again thrice upon him in a sweet and affectionate tone, and slowly open the eyes. Should nothing result, the same experiment must be renewed in the following year, and if necessary a third time, when it is certain that the desired apparition will be obtained, and the longer it has been delayed the more realistic and striking it will be."

"Evocations of knowledge and intelligence are made with more solemn ceremonies. If concerned with a celebrated personage, we must meditate for twenty-one days upon his life and writings, form an idea of his appearance, converse with him mentally, and imagine his answers; carry his portrait, or at least his name, about us; follow a vegetable diet for twenty-one days, and a severe fast during the last

seven. We must next construct the magical oratory. This oratory must be invariably darkened; but if we operate in the daytime, we may leave a narrow aperture on the side where the sun will shine at the hour of the evocation, and place a triangular prism before the opening, and a crystal globe, filled with water, before the prism. If the operation be arranged for the night the magic lamp must be so placed that its single ray shall be upon the alter smoke. The purpose of the preparations is to furnish the magic agent with elements of corporeal appearance, and to ease as much as possible the tension of imagination, which could not be exalted without danger into the absolute illusion of dream. For the rest, it will be easily understood that a beam of sunlight, or the ray of a lamp, colored variously, and falling upon curling and irregular smoke, can in no way create a perfect image. The chafing-dish containing the sacred fire should be in the center of the oratory, and the alter of perfumes close by. The operator must turn toward the east to pray, and the west to invoke; he must be either alone or assisted by two persons preserving the strictest silence; he must wear the magical vestments, which we have described in the seventh chapter and must be crowned with vervain and gold. He should bathe before the operation, and all his under garments must be of the most intact and scrupulous cleanliness. The ceremony should begin with a prayer suited to the genius of the spirit about to be invoked and one which would be approved by him if he still lived. For example, it would be impossible to evoke Voltaire by reciting prayers in the style of St. Bridget. For the great men of antiquity, we may see the hymns of Cleathes or Orpheus, with the adjuration terminating the Golden Venus of Pythagoras. In our own evocation of Apollonius, we used the magical philosophy of Patricius for the ritual, containing the doctrines of Zoroaster and the writings of Hermes Trismegistus. We recited the Nuctemeron of Apollonius in Greek with a loud voice and added the following conjuration,

"Vouchsafe to be present, O Father of All, and thou Thrice Mighty Hermes, Conductor of the dead. Asclepius son of Hephaistus, Patron of the Healing Art; and thou Osiris, Lord of strenght a vigor, do thou thyself be present too. Arnebascenis, Patron of Philosophy, and yet again Asclepius, son of Imuthe, who presidest over poetry.

Apollonius, Apollonius, Apollonius, Thou teachest the Magic of Zoroaster, son of Oromasdes; and this is the worship of the Gods."
~ Eliphas Levi, *'Transcendental Magic, Its Doctrine and Ritual'*, 1896

When looking at the use of libations in connection with honoring the Dead in this example, the Afro-Brazilian spiritual traditions again come to mind, though I will not go into detail here, as there are other skilled Magicians who are covering this subject in length within this compilation. What I will do in place, is shortly examine a related practice of honoring the Dead and working with them in the form of the recently surfaced, though long practiced, Qayinitic tradition of honoring ancestors of Spirit, rather than of blood *(unless applicable)*, which draws its power from praxis very similar to that of the Afro-Brazilian traditions, as well as from Traditional Western Ceremonial structures. In the Holy text of *"Liber Falxifer"*, we see a great fusing of these two different and ancient magical systems into one very solid and powerful manifestation.

Within the Qayinite tradition, libations are given in honor of Holy Qayin, Lord of Death at 12:00am every Monday night. Offerings of Incense, Liquor, Water, Tobacco, Bread, Flowers and Blood are given to the Rebellious One.

These offerings are very similar to the ancient offerings given by the already mentioned Odysseus to the Dead,

> *"When in the underworld, Odysseus begins his Necromantic Arte by first digging a sacrificial pit to hold the libations to be used. Once done he pours a mixture of milk and honey around the pit, followed by sweet wine and finally fresh spring water, all of which are in the end, sprinkled over with barley."*

It is believed by the Cult of Death, *"Templum Falcis Cruentis"*, that Qayin is the son of Samael, and as such, that they are in relation, His son/daughter. However, this lineage does not flow in the form of blood, but of Spirit. In other words, one who is born into a family of Christians can still be of the Holy Blood of Qayin. The link is not a physical one, but one ethereal on the plane of Spirit. Once those of Qayin pass on, they are able to be accessed and worked with as guiding and protective Spirits, assisting the Magician in a great many tasks and situations.

Qayin is also seen as *'The Lord of Death'*, for the slaying of His brother, clay born Abel. He is known as 'The first tiller of the Earth, and first killer of man'. Thus, all of Death's attributes are assigned to Him. Of course as mentioned, there is the Holy Bloodline of Qayin that have passed on into the Spirit realm. When working with the Holy Dead, they must be treated with great honor and respect.

I must say that I am not officially involved with the Temple, but follow many of its recorded traditions. I offer this information only as an overview and study of the Cult of Death and its practices, and not as an official member relaying teachings. I in no way am speaking against the Cult, I honor their ways. However, I also hold the belief that one needs not be an official member of anything, if one is born of the energetic current naturally.

When one begins to contemplate Necromancy, generally it is thought that only the Spirit is brought forth in ritual to commune with. However, there are cases where the *'dead'* body is again infused with a sort of life and spirit, so that communication may be achieved with the living. One ancient Greek example is a tale by Lucan titled *"Pharsalia"* 65 C.E., where the character Erictho reanimates the corpse of a Pompeian soldier by pumping hot blood into it along with magical herbs. Barbarous words are then spoken followed by the evocation of various Underworld deities, causing the soldier's Spirit to appear. The Spirit refuses to possess his now rotting corpse, but is forced inside by the lashings of a snake wielded by Erictho, and with threats to the Spirit concerning the Underworld, which is very reminiscent of the use of *'The Spirit Chain'* in Goetic work, also being of Greek origin.

As well, there is the use of skulls in the Necromantic rites of the Greeks, which is also used in the sacred rites in connection with the Dead, being used as *'Oracles'* for divination, within the praxis of the *"Templum Falcis Cruentis"*. And though there is a history of this, it has been covered well recently in Daniel Schulke's, *"Veneficium"*, and I don't wish to repeat what has already been given.

This idea of a magically revived corpse would fall under the classification of a *'Zombie'*, or the re-animated Dead. These *'Dead'* are brought back to animation magically through various secret rites. Haiti is long known for its history of Walking Dead, William Seabrook, who was an old drinking friend of Aleister Crowley, speaks about tales he had head of Zombies working in sugar fields under the light of the moon while black smoky Spirits circled overhead. Unlike the examples of Greek and English corpse re-animation, the Haitian *'Zombie'* was said to be soulless and unable to speak, thus making it useless for divination.

"...Zombies prayed neither to Papa Legba nor to Brother Jesus, for they were dead bodies walking, without souls or minds"..."But the Zombies shuffled through the market-place, recognizing neither father nor wife, nor mother, and as they turned leftward up the path leading to the graveyard, a woman whose daughter was in the procession of the dead, threw herself screaming before the girls shuffling feet and begged her to stay; but the grave-cold feet of the daughter and the feet of the other dead shuffled over her and onward; and as they approached the graveyard, they began to shuffle faster and rushed among the graves, and each before his own empty grave began clawing at the stones and earth to enter it again; and as their cold hands touched the earth of their own graves, they fell and lay there, rotting carrion."
~ W.B. Seabrook, *'The Magic Island'*, 1929

I must include Seabrook's own personal experience of meeting three *'Zombies'* in a sugar field in the middle of the day, simply because it is so fantastic,

"My first impression of the three supposed 'Zombies', who continued dumbly at work, was that there was something about them unnatural and strange. They were plodding like brutes, like automatons. Without stooping down, I could not fully see their faces, which were bent expressionless over their work. Polynice touched one of them on the shoulder, motioned him to get up. Obediently, like an animal, he slowly stood erect – and what I saw then, coupled with what I had heard previously, or despite it, came as a rather sickening shock. The eyes were the worst. It was not my

imagination. They were in truth like the eyes of a dead man, not blind, but staring, unfocused, unseeing. The whole face, for that matter, was bad enough. It was vacant, as if there was nothing behind it. It seemed not only expressionless, but incapable of expression. I had seen so much previously in Haiti that was outside ordinary normal experience that for the flash of a second I had a sickening, almost panicky lapse in which I thought, or rather felt, 'Great God', maybe this stuff is really true, and if it is true, it is rather awful, for it upsets 'everything'. By 'everything' I meant the natural fixed laws and processes on which all modern human thought and actions are based."
~ W.B. Seabrook, *'The Magic Island'*, 1929

Another fantastic personal account of Necromancy that occurred in Africa which involved the evocation of the Spirit of a fallen king, *(that acted as solid re-animated flesh),* is given by Frederick Kaigh in his book, *"Witchcraft and Magic of Africa", 1947.* He describes a ceremony he witnessed, of a tribe that had lost its king, and needed to evoke him to ask who should be appointed to the then vacant throne. This small series of excerpts speaks of the kings' sudden appearance and the authors amazed reaction in response,

"Nkatosi, the chief with whose corpse I had but a few hours since encountered so much trouble, is sitting quite unconcernedly on his throne. I did not see him come, but I saw him there as plainly as I can this sunny afternoon see the policeman on his beat outside my window. Everyone present sees him as clearly as I do."..."With all too vivid memories of the recently seen, vile and stinking corpse, I feel none too well at this demonstration."..."For the first time he rises, and for the first time, his feet actually touch the earth. After that he makes no more sound, and from that moment he gradually begins to look less material as it

were. He turns away from the people to face the moon, and it is then that, for the first time, we see the dim outline of the horrid bashed-in wound in the back of the skull. He walks slowly and majestically down the lane of the moon, and thus, naturally and simply, sets out on his long lost journey."
~ Frederick Kaigh, *"Witchcraft and Magic of Africa"*, 1947

Though this is clearly an account of true Necromancy, the Spirit called forth was able to take on a completely solid form without entering its physical *'dead'* body. This is reminiscent of Levi's account of the seeing and being touched by the Spirit Apollonius in full physical form. These examples should be seen and remembered as a warning to the Magician, as to the strength the Dead possess and wield.

There are other dangers to be warned of. When working with the Dead, some ancient Necromancers believed they must meet them *'halfway'*, that is, in a middle ground between the world of the living, and that of the dead. They would leave their body in order to travel to the Underworld, or close to it. The danger presented here, is the Magician being drawn too close the Spirit world, and then not having the strength to return to their living bodies, thus being fated to join the ranks of the Dead themselves. As well, let us not forget the warning words of Lovecraft's Necromancer, Jedediah Orne of Salem,

"I say to you againe, doe not call up Any that you can not put downe; by the which I meane, Any that can in Turne call up somewhat against you, whereby your Powerfullest Devices may not be of use. Ask of the Lesser, least the Greater shall not wish to answer, and shall commande more than you"

~ H.P. Lovecraft, *'The Case of Charles Dexter Ward'*, 1943

I have felt that a bit of background was needed on this subject of Necromancy, though I also wish to contribute to this forbidden Arte in the form of a single ritual derived from ancient traditions, and infused with new concepts. Looking at Necromancy through scientific/magical eyes, I analyze the mechanics of the Arte and look to isolate the methods *(that resonate with me)*, that make it work. As Frazier would say,

> *"...to draw out the few simple threads of which the tangled skein is composed; to disengage the abstract principles from their concrete applications; in short, to discern the spurious science behind the bastard art."*
> ~ *'The Golden Bough'*, 1890

I have found that as with most all rituals, it is the culminating of energy that ensures the success of a Necromantic rite. One must have obtained, or generated enough power to reach through the barriers of the worlds and make contact with the entity intended. Often times, this is done before the ritual even begins, though through ritual, great energy is also brought up and directed at the intended contact and communication. It is known that adjusting one's energy to a specific current is also of great help in ensuring this success. As an example, when working with Lovecraftian Entities, one should immerse themselves in that particular current by reading Lovecraft, meditating in twilight while speaking the entities names with intent to be heard, and of course practicing various forms of Lovecraftian *'Fringe'* Magic such as is presented in *"Volubilis Ex Chaosium"*.

When working with the Death Current, one must align themselves with this energy as well. Personally because I work with Chthonic Spirits regularly, I wear a 300 year old coffin nail around my neck at all times, to help me keep in touch with this current. As well, when working with the Dead and Chthonic Spirits I use an oak wand that was ritually harvested from an ancient gallows tree. These items in combination with other 300 year old coffin nails, graveyard soil and bones of the Fallen, create a concentration of Death energy that powers any rite involving communication with the Dead.

Necromancy is a little known art, leaving many areas open for the Necromancer to experiment with and study. Its history is ancient and hidden, shrouded away from the light of normalcy and *'Natural Law'*. There are many reasons one would utilize this dark art, but perhaps its use is truly based on our curiosity to know what lies ahead of us. For the darkness will indeed come and claim us all, we are in this very moment, being stalked by Death. He is behind you, to your left. And, once we are *'gone'*, perhaps someone will call us up, ask us of our knowledge, of our times and life. The following ritual is accessible to all who wish to utilize it. However, in the great spirit of Lovecraft, this rite is also intended for my personal use…I ask the ancestors of my true bloodline, that I call to through these written words, across the seas of time that now separate us, to use this ritual to call me up once I have *'gone'*, to raise me from this blackened earth once again…for I will come…

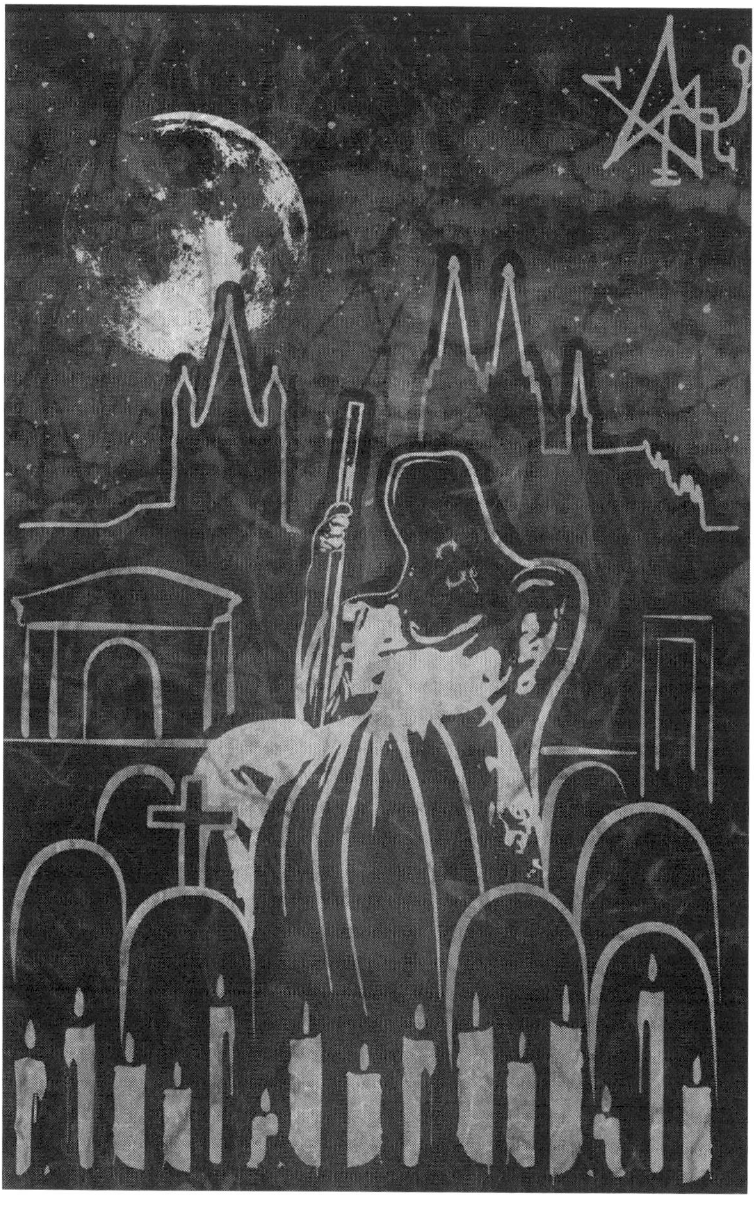

Drawing Forth The Dead; *'The Necromantic Ritual of Re-Awakening'*

The Necromantic ritual being presented here is based on the various methods of Necromancy discussed throughout this piece. It brings together the effective elements needed to generate the power to push through the barriers that lie between the world of the living, and that of the Dead. It is designed to raise a great amount of energy, while simultaneously descending the Necromancer into a deep state of consciousness. In this manner, the Necromancer is ritually descending down into the Underworld, while the Dead are being raised up from out of it, creating a ritual space of twilight, *'halfway'* between the worlds.

This ritual should be held indoors in a large area, or partially indoors if there are holes in the roofing and walls. It should take place somewhere abandoned, forgotten with time, somewhere deserted or decayed where memories linger as dust upon an untrodden floor. A place like a forgotten warehouse, in the basement of an old house, in the attic of a strange factory, somewhere that is scarcely frequented, but that once was, would be ideal.

The Necromantic Circle is best made using white chalk, as it will not be disturbed when the Necromancer travels the descending staircase into 'the spaces between', though crushed eggshells or flour may be utilized. The circle is 12ft. in diameter. At 4 ½ ft in from the outer edge of the circle, another circle is drawn with a diameter of 3ft. All edges of the inner circle should be 4 ½ ft, from the edges of the outer circle, placing it in the direct center of the larger circle. Locate the North of the large circle using a compass, and begin a spiral pattern counter-clockwise or widdershins around the inside of the large circle three times, ending at the North edge of the smaller circle. Starting again at the top or North edge of the large circle where the spiral begins, start sectioning off areas as you travel the spiral inward, making each section slightly smaller than the last. The last section should not be smaller than the size of the Necromancer's foot. On each of the sections or steps, a pentagram is to be drawn so that they face the inner circle the Necromancer is to work in. This is done to infuse the circle with energy and strength. From the inside of the inner circle looking out, the Necromancer is surrounded by empowering pentagrams, while from outside the circle, they are seen as protective pentacles.

When done, the circle creates the illusion of a descending spiral staircase that ends in a small circular 3ft. area, where the Magician will call up the Dead and hold congress with whichever Spirit he has called forth.

The Necromantic Triangle of Evocation should also be drawn out with white chalk as mentioned with the circle. And like the circle, it also measures 12ft. from its apex pentagram (turned facing the North of the circle), to its base lying between the two adjacent pentagrams that help form the second and third points of the triangle *(see illustration)*. Once the Necromantic Triangle has been drawn, a 3ft. circle is to be drawn centered inside. This is known as the Spirit Circle where libations of blood are offered.

This rite represents the journey into the Underworld, the descent into darkness, into an un-natural silence, where the Necromancer travels into the land of the Dead, and is able to hear their gossamer whispers. This symbolic descent into the Underworld is reminiscent of the ancient rite of walking a labyrinth, as Thomas Karlsson points out,

"The paths of the labyrinth will deeply influence the mind. It is claimed that these labyrinths are pictures of the mind and the brain. To enter these ancient stone labyrinths is a form of initiation. It stages an entry into the centre of the Underworld where the core of the soul and secret of existence; the diamond, can be found."
~ Thomas Karlsson, *'Uthark; Nightside of the Runes'*, 2002

The praxis of Traveling around the Magical Circle counterclockwise, or widdershins, is drawn from an inversion of an ancient rite practiced in Freemasonry called *'Circumambulation'*. An initiate is led around the temple clockwise three times to honor the *'Grand Architect'* of the Universe. Here where it is used, it represents the un-natural flow of natural laws, and in effect, is a direct rebellious act directed at the *'Grand Architect'*. Bringing the Dead back to life is an un-natural act and not what is *'meant to be'*. Necromancy goes against the Natural Order. It is interesting to note that this act of *'Circumambulation'* has been traced back to ancient Pagan Roman times, making its utilization here a complementary fit.

Libations of milk & honey, blood, red roses, and myrrh incense, are to be given in two different ways depending on your location. If outside, pour the mixture of milk and honey around the pit or Spirit Circle dug in the Triangle. The blood of course is to be drained into the earthen pit, and the roses are to be placed around the very edge of the pit. If inside, pour the mixture of milk and honey around the Spirit Circle designated for the offerings. Once done, utilize a clean black bowl for the blood offered, and place it in the center of the Spirit Circle surrounded by the red roses. The myrrh incense should be burning just inside all three points of the Necromantic Triangle, there should be enough placed there to burn for a good length of time. An oak wand, scepter is needed for this rite, as oak is the wood of the Crossroads. As well, if you are contacting a specific Spirit, some of their personal belongings are to be placed within the Necromantic Triangle. As tradition would have it, a sword is utilized as well to protect the Necromancer of unwanted Spirits, and drive off those who would do harm.

Begin the rite at midnight. The Necromantic Circle and Triangle as well as all offerings should already be in their place, and all incense lit. Use whatever candles are necessary to provide dim lighting. Begin standing outside of the circle, facing its North side, so your back is to the triangle. Once there, take a deep breath, and know it is the last one you will take in the world of the living, until you again return outside of the circle. When your mind is clear of all internal dialogue, begin by taking your first step. As each step is taken, trace over the pentagrams on each step with your oak scepter infusing them with power. The Magician slows his breathing, clears his mind, and sinks into a deeper level of consciousness with each step, so that when finally arriving at the inner/bottom platform of calling, he is attuned to the energy being worked with, and ready to begin the rite. The journey *'down'* should be slow and steady.

Once at the bottom, in the Circle of Calling, sit down, close your eyes and meditate on the blackness that surrounds you. Your wand should be in your left hand, your sword in your right. Feel the cold of the night upon your skin, feel the Spirits of the Underworld already begin to draw near in anticipation of the rite shortly to begin. Open your eyes and call to them, bring them forth, though they can be dangerous, their presence strengthens the rite. The words are whispered softly with Intent, not forceful with Will.

They are spoken slowly with meaning. When you feel it is time, begin,

"Dark Spirits of forever night,

Sinestral Shades of liquid soot,

Hear my words…

I call you…

Gather round from forsaken nether realms,

Draw near…

Know the warmth of my living voice upon your cold dead ears,

Know my Spirit that calls yours from across the Void,

Phantasmal whispers of Twilights Shade,

Hear my words…

I call you…

Lost Specters of Midnight's Garden,

Damned Souls of Luna's light,

Draw near…

For the Darkness that ever surrounds you..,

Is ever within me…"

Once spoken three times with devotion, the Necromancer is ready to call forth the intended Spirit of their choosing. Here I leave it to the Necromancer to develop their own oration to the lost one they wish to speak with. It is important to remember to be direct with your wording, and patient for a response.

Upon completion of the rite, thank the Spirit for attending and working with you, inform it that you have no more to say at this time, and that it is again free to wander in the mists. When you feel it has departed, stand and address the Chthonic Spirits that still surround and thank them for attending as well, but that you now ask them to depart and to do you no harm, as you are protected under the name of the Dark One, Samael.

Proceed slowly back *'up'* the stairs to the living world of man. As each step is taken, slowly raise your consciousness from out of the meditative state is has been in. Before leaving the circle make the sign of the pentagram in the air in front of you, and cross back out of the Necromantic Circle. The rite is finished…

VENVS OBSCVRA MMXXI

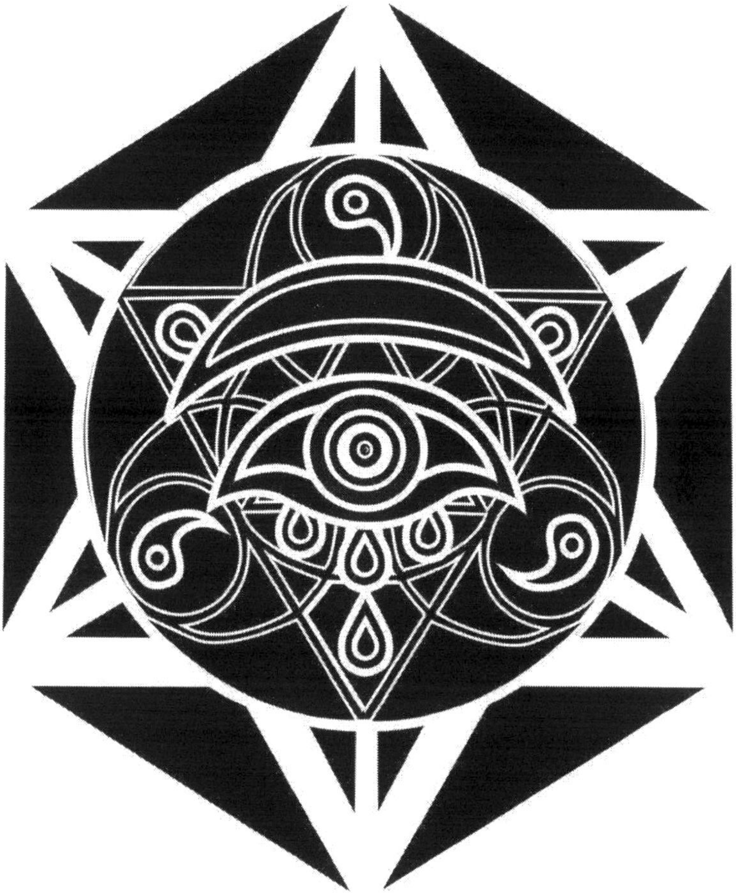

The Crawling Chaos Of Infinite Form; *'Nyarlathotep'*

Who or what is Nyarlathotep ? The soul of the Old Ones, The Messenger, The Crawling Chaos ? One could define him as the all-encompassing unholy spirit of his reality, equivalent, though opposite to that of the Judeo/Christian Holy Spirit or Christ. For Nyarlathotep is the messenger and soul of the Dark Gods made manifest unto men in the form of a man, the son of Azathoth, God of Chaos, King of Kings. For it is known that all of earth's Gods kneel before 'Him', the Alpha and the Omega… *"I Am The Last"*.

It is in this comparison that one may alternatively equate Nyarlathotep with Tawuse Melek/Melek Taus who is also known as Shaitan. Much has been written of the Yezidi cult of Northern Iraq and their connections to Shaitan, so detail will not ensue. However, contained within their scriptures is what is known as the *"Kitab Al-Jilwah"*, written in the twelfth century and translated as, *"Book of Revelation"* or *"Book of Divine Effulgence"*. It begins with a familiar statement, *"I Was, Am Now, and Shall Have No End"* which one can easily compare to Lovecraft's famous quote in his short story, *"The Dunwitch Horror"*, which is *"The Old Ones Were, The Old Ones Are, And The Old Ones Shall Be"*.

There are alternate realities and dimensions, spaces "In-Between". Could not Nyarlathotep be the Shaitan of his reality, which has now intersected and conjoined with ours by means of *'Strange Angles'* ? Is not the force and essence of Chaos that exists in the realm of other dimensions, joined in blood to the force of Chaos of our own ? Are they not the same ? Nyarlathotep is described by Lovecraft as appearing as a pharaoh of the Old Blood:

> *"Who he was, none could tell, but he was of the old native blood and looked like a Pharaoh...And it was then that Nyarlathotep came out of Egypt...Into the lands of civilization came Nyarlathotep, swarthy, slender, and sinister...He said he had risen up out of the blackness of twenty-seven centuries, and that he had heard messages from places not on this planet"*
> ~ H.P. Lovecraft, 'Nyarlathotep', 1920

He could also be seen as a manifestation of Set, the Egyptian god of darkness and chaos who has obvious connections with Satan/Lucifer. By Frank G. Ripel's description in "The Magic of Atlantis", Nyarlathotep is known as a bringer of light, whose face is so bright that it blinds all those who would look upon it,

> *"Nyarlathotep manifested himself in human form, as a tall man with hairs of fire and wrapped in a long red mantle; and he was wearing a singular Crown, a Golden Circle with the symbol of that which one day will be called the Sun, and from the shoulders two Golden Snakes were bending above his head. Nobody could gaze unto his Flaming Face without becoming totally blind."*

The golden snakes on Nyarlathotep's shoulders are interesting to note. The Hebrew word for serpent, *'Nachash'*, translates as 'A Shining One', which again connects Lucifer with Nyarlathotep and his flaming face/eyes. But also to the force of Chaos itself, in that it is often represented as a snake winding its way ever through the restrictions of Order, thus causing needed change and illumination. Lucifer/Samael seduced man from ignorance into illumination and thus damnation, just as Nyarlathotep spread his sinister gnosis across the land enlightening the chosen, while destroying the ignorant,

> *"He spoke much of the sciences – of electricity and psychology – and gave exhibitions of power which sent his spectators away speechless, yet which swelled his fame to exceeding magnitude. Men advised each other to see Nyarlathotep, and shuddered."*
> ~H.P. Lovecraft, *'Nyarlathotep'*, 1920

Though Nyarlathotep can appear as 'shinning', he also can don the appearance of a dark or black skinned with Caucasian features, as he does possess many forms. There wad a report of a tall, sleek 'Black Man' with flaming eyes that came through Milan Italy, who left chaos in his wake. There was a prophesized event that foretold of Milan being poisoned by the Devil in 1630, and it was. The plague swept through the land and had reached Milan in 1629, but the events that occurred there are quite curious,

> *"...All the doors in the principal streets of the city were marked with a curious daub, or spot, as if a sponge, filled with purulent matter of the plague sores, had been pressed against them.".*
> ~ Giuseppe Ripamonti, *'De peste Mediolani quae fuit anno'*, 1630, 1640

The Devil was said to have taken up residence in the city,

> *"He had taken a house in Milan, in which he prepared his poisonous unguents, and furnished them to his emissaries for distribution".*
> ~ Giuseppe Ripamonti, *'De peste Mediolani quae fuit anno'*, 1630, 1640

One man apparently with nothing to lose, confronted this *'Devil'*, and this is a partial description of that encounter,

"...A tall stranger of a majestic aspect; his long black hair floated in the wind – Fire flashed from his large black eyes, and a curl of ineffable scorn dwelt upon his lips. The look of the stranger was so sublime that he was awed, and trembled with fear when he gazed upon him. His complexion was much darker than that of any man he had ever seen, and the atmosphere around him was hot and suffocating. He perceived immediately that he was a being of another world."
~ Giuseppe Ripamonti, *'De peste Mediolani quae fuit anno'*, 1630, 1640

Lovecraft's description of Nyarlathotep in *"The Dreams of the Witch House"* is very similar, describing him as,

"A tall, lean man of dead black colouration but without the slightest sign of negroid features: wholly devoid of either hair or beard, and wearing as his only garment a shapeless robe of some heavy black fabric. His feet were indistinguishable because of the table and bench, but he must have been shod, since there was a clicking whenever he changed position. The man did not speak, and bore no trace of expression on his small, regular features. He merely pointed to a book of prodigious size which lay open on the table..."

Milan of course was taken by the plague, the confronting man in the account was said to have prayed to god, thus vanquishing 'The Black Man'. Though, I'm fairly certain that it was the majestic stranger who truly had his way, as devastation was all that was left in his wake.

"And where Nyarlathotep went, rest vanished; for the small hours were rent with the screams of nightmare..."
~ H.P. Lovecraft, 'Nyarlathotep', 1920

The similarities between Nyarlathotep and Aiwass, the entity that contacted Aleister Crowley, has also been noted by researcher Peter Smith, who writes,

> *"Nyarlathotep's physical appearance also compares quite strikingly to that of the Astral entity, Aiwaz, who communicated the text known as "The Book of the Law" to Aleister Crowley in Cairo, 1904, thus inaugurating the present Aeon of Horus."*
> ~ Nameless Aeons, 1999

Crowley's description of Aiwass is very interesting as it mirrors almost exactly Lovecraft's depiction of Nyarlathotep, as well as Ripamonti's account of the 'Devil' in Milan, most notably the power that resides within the eyes, In "The Equinox of the God", Crowley described how he saw Aiwass,

> *"Aiwass with a body composed of fine matter, having a gauze-like transparency…He seemed to be a tall, dark man in his thirties, well-knit, active and strong, with the face of a savage king, and eyes veiled lest their gaze should destroy what they saw. The dress was not Arab; it suggested Assyria or Persia, but very vaguely."*

Some have even suggested that Lovecraft and Crowley somehow knew each other due to the fact that there are so many similarities between the two concerning magical praxis and philosophy. This, of course, is highly unlikely and founded on misinformation. However, there is a connection that lies in plain sight…Nyarlathotep/Aiwass. This being came and spoke to each of them, whispering secrets that would *(and will)* change the world.

Another strong connection that Nyarlathotep shares with Lucifer is the Witches Sabbat,

> *"There was the immemorial figure of the deputy or messenger of hidden and terrible powers – the 'Black Man' of the witch cult, and the 'Nyarlathotep' of the "Necronomicon"...The Witches Sabbath wad drawing near. May Eve was Walpurgis Night, when Hell's blackest evil roamed the earth and all the slaves of Satan gathered for nameless rites and deeds."*
> ~ H.P. Lovecraft, *'The Dreams in the Witch House'*, 1932

Here Lovecraft clearly shows thar Nyarlathotep and Lucifer are synonymous, and are one and the same, or at least interchangeable. The ceremony of signing Azathoth's black book in blood at the Sabbat is identical to accounts of the Witch's Sabbat where one also makes a pact with the Devil in blood.

> *"He must meet the Black Man, and go with them all to the throne of Azathoth at the center of ultimate Chaos...He must sign in his own blood the book of Azathoth and take a new secret name..."*
> ~ H.P. Lovecraft, *'The Dreams in the Witch House'*, 1932

Nyarlathotep has more in common with Lucifer, Shaitan, Aiwass and Set than one might initially recognize. All are anthropomorphic representations of the great energy of Chaos manifested into deific forms, the energy of the Great Daemon Sultan Azathoth.

In this new light of speculation, the 'Fall' of the Old Ones is quite similar to Lucifer and the fall of the rebel Angels in that they were both abandoned to the earth and the Spaces In-Between which they haunt as monstrous ghosts in twilight dimensions. The fall of the Old Ones was written of by Lovecraft and Derleth, in "The Lurker at the Threshold, 1945,

"And to His brothers it happen'd likewise, that they were tak'n by Those whom They defy'd and hurled into banishment..."
~ The Lurker at the Threshold, 1945

One look through the Goetia and the descriptions therein of the demons that are to be called forth into materialization, leads one to see a natural similarity between their numerous and conjoined forms, and those that are the Old Ones. One such example is the demon Bael,

"He appeareth in divers shapes, sometimes like a cat, sometimes like a toad, and sometimes like a man, and sometimes all these forms at once."
~ Ars Goetia from the Lesser Key of Solomon Lemegeton

A similar sense of monstrosity is conveyed in Lovecraft's description of Cthulhu as,

"An octopus, a dragon, and a human caricature…A pulpy, tentacled head surmounted a grotesque and scaly body with rudimentary wings"
~ H.P. Lovecraft, *'The Call of Cthulhu'*, 1926

Lovecraft often spoke of various beings as 'indescribable' in his accounts, and has been criticized for his lack of imagination. However, Ronove – the 27th spirit and Bifrons – the 46th spirit of the Goetia, are simply described as *'Monsters'*. Given that the author/s of the Goetia could describe the other infinitely different and fantastic demons with seemingly no problem, the term, *'Monster'* seems to be a term interchangeable with that of *'Indescribable'*. Not all things can be described in words alone, and would only confuse if attempted. Artful images such as Hieronymus Bosch's *'Hell'* or *'The Last Judgement'* from the sixteenth century, reflect the similarity between the descriptions and monstrosities of fallen angels and that of the fallen Old Ones.

Nyarlathotep is the messenger between the Old Ones and mankind, the one who opens the interdimensional gate called Yog-Sothoth. In this aspect he could be compared to Papa Legba of the Vodoun tradition, know as *'Lord of the Crossroads'*. Papa Legba is the opener of the gate that facilitates interaction between man and the Lwa, leading to a direct connection with death, and the Nightside of the Qabalistic Tree of Life, which houses the *'Tunnels of Set'*, or in Yog-Sothery, the *'Vaults of Zin'*.

Nyarlathotep is known as the Crawling Chaos and can assume many forms, sometimes all at once. The title perfectly describes the flow of energy that is embodied by the Left Hand Path, slithering and winding through order, causing a break down of the perfect system. It causes decay and death, and thus rebirth of new forms and paths that are free of the orderly, locked down control that has kept mankind repressed and restrained.

> *"I Am The Last...I Will Tell The Audient Void"*
> ~ Nyarlathotep

These words bring with them such a tone of sadness. There is despair in the voice in which words are spoken out of importance of the moment, rather than for another to hear. A speaking of one's own name and title to remind that they still 'are', after all has gone.

> *"I Am The Last..."*

There is so much solitude in the Abyss.

"I Will Tell The Audient Void..."

One last duty to be performed for the sake of completion, though He will be the only witness of this act of closure. For Nyarlathotep is indeed, *'The Last'*. The last of what and when, no one knows, Though one receives the feeling that this is indeed a finality, the end. He is the one who was in the 'beginning' and will remain the one in the end, the Alpha and Omega, created to observe, as the concentrated manifestation of what are known as the Old Ones.

They say that between madness and genius there lies a fine line that is easily crossed, a path traversed without notice, where one looks up, and finds that they are indeed on the other side of the looking glass, though possess no recollection of having made the journey. Nyarlathotep is that fine line, more often riding on the wings of madness than those of sanity. Once men have made his acquaintance, they often find themselves in a dream like state, walking over the edge of reality, into the swirling vortex of creation, never to return. It was their thirst for knowledge that drove them to this point of no return. Their curiosity of the possibility to *'Know'* of secret things, the forbidden, the apple of knowledge and of truth hung before them, tempting them to have one sweet bite. Once the eyes have been opened, and truth is embraced, it often overwhelms and sends reason to a place it cannot exist, thus shattering it. However, for those born of Chaos, it is possible to embrace the secrets that lie in the shadow and truly *'Know'* Nyarlathotep, the wildest and most untamed of the anthropomorphic facets of Chaos. Nyarlathotep, Set, Lucifer and Aiwass are all manifested forms that the chaotic energy Nyarlathotep has taken to communicate and shed black flame of gnosis upon those born of the same energy. For those who are of the children of Lucifer, are also of the children of Nyarlathotep...

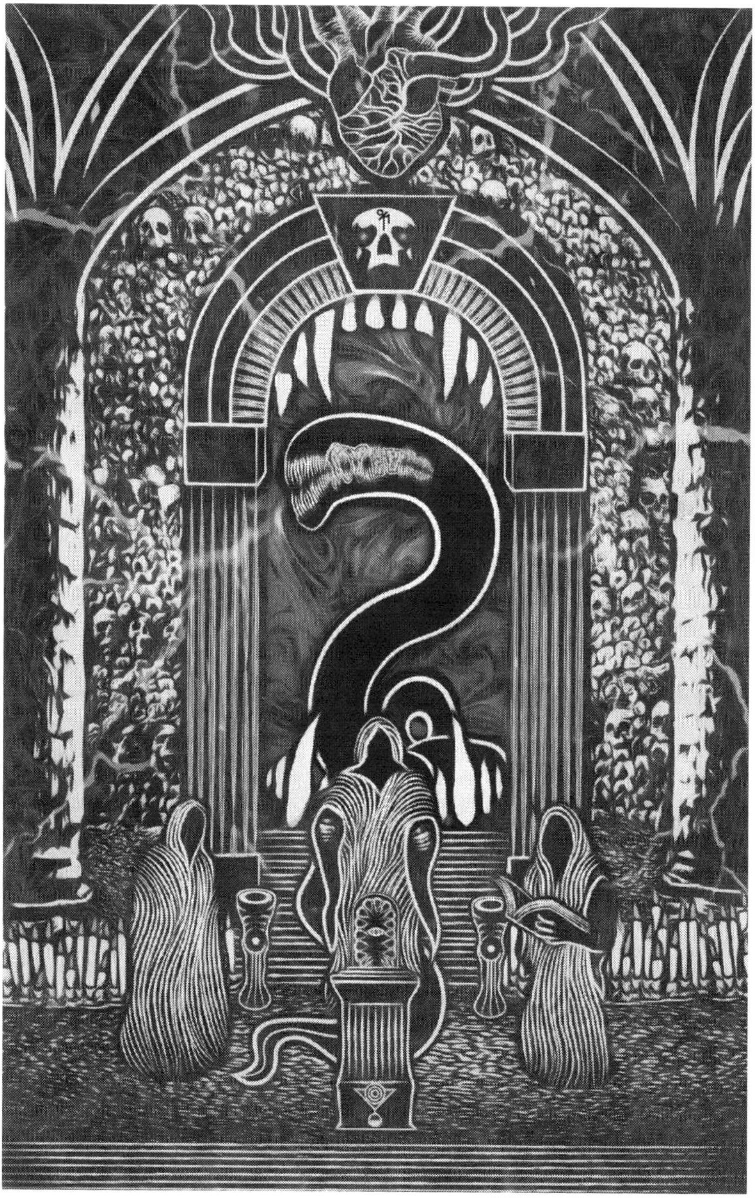

Consuming The Blackened Serpent

This is an essential meditation exercise that is intended to connect the magician with the pure black snake current of Nyarlathotep. Here, he is seen and worked with as the Blackened Serpent, representing Chaos. This meditation is to be held outside at dusk, in a dry desert-like location that is quiet and where you will not be disturbed. You will need a red candle and small bowl of consecrated water. Find your place by walking the area and feeling which specific spot will be suitable for your work. Do not rush this process, it is very important to locate the 'right' area to perform the ritual.

Once you have found a proper working space, create a circle upon the ground, nine feet in diameter, create it out of whatever natural material is available to you, such as rocks or branches. Pour the consecrated water into a clean bowl, and stand outside the circle with the bowl before you. State your intent clearly:

"Let this circle of arte be empowered and cleansed by the shadow of these dark waters of the In-Between !"

Sprinkle the sacred water in the closed circle with your first and middle fingers *(keeping a small amount of water on the side for later use)* Place your fingers upon your forehead where the third eye is situated, rest and state out loud:

"Let this vessel of flesh be cleansed and prepared for the spirit of the Blackened Snake that winds His way through this reality !"

Walk into the circle of art and sit down legs crossed. Slow the beat of your heart by breathing deeply. Light the red candle and place it within the edge of the circle, directly in front of you, making sure to place the sacred water bowl to its left, and state:

"Burning flame of Yog-Sothoth, ignite the fires in the realms of Twilight and permit passage into this world from Spaces In-Between !"

Dig the earth and put a small amount of soil in the palm of each of your hands, resting your hands face up upon your knees. Connect with the earth and the air. Close your eyes and meditate, clearing your mind of all internal dialogue. Visualize a black hole about six inches in diameter just below the center of your chest, where your solar plexus is located. Visualize yourself as a shell, empty, with only a hole leading to your core. Now visualize a black snake directly facing you, about six feet in front of the circle. Lock eyes with the serpent, 'see' it and connect with it, inviting it in. Watch as it slithers silently towards you. The circle here is not to keep the entity out, but to concentrate its energy into a purified area, so it will have no trouble crossing through the boundary. Stopping inches from you and raising its head up to the level of the hole in your chest, you feel its head entering your body and its black scales sliding into you. As it enters you, it is coiling into the hole you have visualized, filling your entire chest cavity. Feel its weight and strength.

When the serpent has finished coiling inside you, feel it growing in strength, pulsating as it draws strength from you in waves, getting stronger, then leveling out, until you no longer hold it back. When it has nearly drained you of all power, it will burst forth from you, dispersing its strength throughout your limbs, filling your empty shell with its unworldly black force. Leaving your body, it will shed its skin, its essence taking up residence within you. Visualize the abundant energy flowing from the hole where it exited, covering your whole body. The energy expands across your chest in all directions, quickly flowing over your stomach, around and up your back, up and down each of your legs through your feet, over your shoulders and down each of your arms through your hands and fingers. Feel it race up your neck, over your face and through your hair. Open your mouth and drink it in, it has washed over and through you. You are now cleansed and filled with the power and essence of the Blackened Serpent that is Nyarlathotep. Open your eyes. You now hold the primal forces of Chaos within.

This meditation is very powerful and leaves one 'seeing' the world in a different way. It is recommended that this rite be performed every three months to re-energize and align yourself with the black current of Chaos. This rite is also significant in that it connects the magician to the five earthly elements in a method agreeable to Left Hand Path practitioners. Cthulhu is represented through the use of water, Shub-Niggurath through the earth, Azathoth by air, Yog-Sothoth by fire, and Nyarlathotep by spirit, encompassing them all.

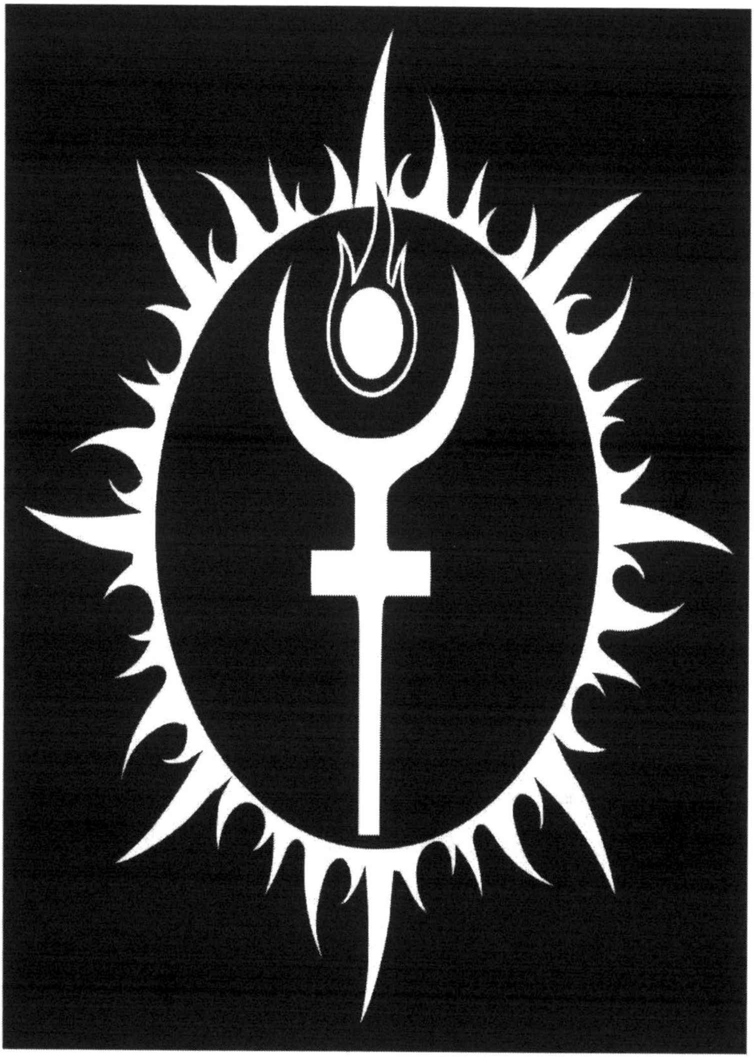

The Sonic Structure Of Incantations; *'Vibration Is Key'*

The use of incantations, evocations, invocations and the like, all stem from the same base science of vibrating Intent of the sorcerer from their personal subjective reality into the shared reality all can agree upon, causing the desired change to occur. In other words, the sorcerer *'pushes'* their Intent from their *'Personal Reality Grid'* into the *'Consensual Reality Matrix'* through the use of Intent and vibration to cause a change all can experience and agree on. This science is used when calling upon a particular spiritual entity; names have power because they are a specific vibration sequence or pattern that is connected to the entity being called forth. A spiritual entities name is as powerful and connected to it as its magical seal or sigil,

> *"The essential character of things and men resides in their names. Therefore, to know a name is to be privy to the secret of its owners being, and master of his fate. The members of many primitive tribes have two names, one for public use, the other jealously concealed, known only to the man who bears it."... "To know the name of a man is to exercise power over him alone; to know the name of a higher, supernatural being is to dominate the entire province over which that being presides. The more such names a magician has garnered, the greater the number of spirits that are subject to his call and command. This simple theory is at the bottom of the magic which operates through the mystical names and words that are believed to control the forces which in turn control our world. The spirits guarded their names as jealously as ever did a primitive tribe."*

~ Jewish Magic and Superstition, 1939

Though it is not the name itself that is important, but the names particular vibration into *'reality'* that is of importance. Vibration is key in magical systems as it excites and releases the static energy that is built up within the entwined angles that compose the Triangles of Arte used in various magical systems and carries the Intent of the sorcerer into the consensual reality. Sound has always been defined as a wave, and while true, this term does not accurately describe how sound actually behaves. Sound waves exist as vibrations of pressure in a medium such as air and water. They are created by the vibration of an object, which causes the molecules within the air surrounding that object to vibrate. The vibrating air then causes the human eardrum to in turn vibrate, which the brain translates as sound. Sound is an expanding bubble made up of one existing connected wave, it is vibration composed of pure energy. The energy excites the molecules around it causing them to in turn vibrate, starting a chain reaction to occur until the molecules have lost all their excitement the farther away they get from the source, resulting eventually in *'silence'*. The audio pressures or vibrations upon the triangle of arte excite the compacted static energy within the angles, until an apex is reached and the energy released, much as in sexual orgasm. Here lies the process of frustration, excitation and release. This type of hyper-sexual frustration is especially seen within the polygon of the trapezoid, unable to connect with its missing counterpart (the triangle) creating union, and streamlining the flow of energy contained within.

Contrary to popular belief, there are no exact or correct words to be said in a spell. All that is important is that the sorcerer fully infuse their words with emotion and intent. When this is done in conjunction with vibration, the sorcerer imprints his intent onto and into the Consensual Reality Matrix and changes the coding, or structure for an outcome that was personally desired and would not under normal circumstances come to pass. This is magic. This is reality manipulation. Deep vibrations of sorcerous Intent make more of an impact and get better results as the energy is imprinted more deeply into reality . Though this varies as there are times a sorcerer's Intent can be so strong that their words can be whispered and still have devastating effect.

> *"It is not known to me whether any of my readers have witnessed any kind of magical ceremony, or heard an invocation recited by a skilled practitioner – though I should say that few have. The tone always adopted is one which will yield the maximum vibration. For many students a deep intoning, or humming, is one which vibrates the most."*
> ~ Israel Regardie

An example of the use of pure emotional vibration can be seen in grimoires such as *"Tuba Veneris: Libellus Veneri Nigro Sacer"* that use barbarous words of power. The words themselves have no meaning, they are solely there to be used as a vibrational vehicle upon which the sorcerer's Intent travels. In such rites, pure vibration and Intent is all that is needed to accomplish the ritual being performed.

> *"Long lists of divine names and words of Power, sometimes called Barbarous Words pf Power, were recited in the form of litanies. In the Clavicle of Solomon revealed to Ptolemy we find the instruction that once the magician had recited all these names with the utmost devotion one was advised: "Heare let the maiesty of god cum in". The implication is that by calling upon the hierarchy of divine names, the operator was invoking these specific aspects og*

God's holy power and focusing it into the magic circle and thus bringing it into the person therein."
~ William Kiesel

It is clear that even though the forces being called forth in this example originate in Order, the base science remains the same; a pattern of vibration is laid down as the vehicle, while the emotional Intent is the passenger. Another example of this can be seen in H.P. Lovecraft's works. His use of seemingly unpronounceable names for the Old Ones and their evocations is well known. He has maximized the vibrational science so contact is more easily made between intelligences. I have featured his barbarous words in the Yog-Sothoth evocation within "The Black Book of Azathoth",

*"I call out to,
And into,
The primordial absolute chaos of the
Darkened abyss,
I call to the endless void of absolute
silent black,
That lies in the deep waters of cold truth,
I call you,
To bring 'Him' forth…
I call to the All-In-One and One-In-All,
The all seeing one who dwells in the
Negative light of cold understanding,
I call to you Beyond One,
Into this dark temple to become the gate,
I call Yog-Sothoth !
I call the gate keeper !
Come forth Yog-Sothoth !
Yog-Sothoth knows the gate,
Yog-Sothoth is Key and guardian of the gate !
Yog-Sothoth you are now called*

*forth to take the form of the Trinity
of Triangles,
To manifest as the Three-In-Nine
And become the Triangles,
So I may answer Their call,
And so they may answer mine !
Yog-Sothoth I call you to manifest
As the Trinity of Triangles,
Yog-Sothoth become the gateway between !
Yog-Sothoth become !*

*N'gai ~ n'gha'ghaa ~ bugg-shoggog
Y'hah; Yog-Sothoth…*

*N'gai ~ n'gha'ghaa ~ bugg-shoggog
Y'hah; Yog-Sothoth…*

*N'gai ~ n'gha'ghaa ~ bugg-shoggog
Y'hah; Yog-Sothoth…*

Ygnaih ~ Ygniih ~ Thflthkh'ngha

Yog-Sothoth,

Y'bthnk ~ H'ehye ~ N'grkdl'h…

Ygnaih ~ Ygniih ~ Thflthkh'ngha

Yog-Sothoth,

Y'bthnk ~ H'ehye ~ N'grkdl'h…

Yi-nash-Yog-Sothoth-he-lgeb-fi-throdog Yah !

Yi-nash-Yog-Sothoth-he-lgeb-fi-throdog Yah !

Yi-nash-Yog-Sothoth-he-lgeb-fi-throdog Yah !

Let The Gateway Be Opened !

Again, we see such seemingly random compilations of letters also with the Enochian magical system, where the names of the angels are based on a vocal system that is vibrated such as the Enochian Keys or Calls. Also in the Enochian system we see those vocal vibrations being used in conjunction with the sigil di Emeth or the sigil of truth which contains angles of frustration containing static energy. And, in the controversial *"Tuba Veneris: Libellus Veneri Nigro Sacer"* of the 16th century *(as mentioned before)*, also said to be of Dr. John Dee's hand, we see again the use of barbarous words in the invocations given for the spirits. Here is an example of the invocation given for the spirit *'Mogarip'*,

"Mogarip! Mogarip! Mogarip!

Hamka Temach Algazoth Syrath

Amilgos Murzocka Imgat

Alaja Amgustaroth Horim Suhaja

Mogarip! Mogarip! Mogarip!"

As well, within the Voodoo/Vodoun systems the heavy vibration of drums is utilized to excite and transmit the Intent and emotion of the masses to the Lwa they are attempting to contact. An amazing firsthand account of a Vodoun rite which incorporated the use of drums, is given by Richard Loederer in his book *"Voodoo Fire in Haiti"*, published 1935,

"As we rode through the night, the drums were beating again – but with a new rhythm that I had never heard before. I was keyed up to a pitch of perspiring excitement, fearing what was to come and yet unwilling to turn back. We were about to participate in a monstrous performance, an orgy which one white man in a million has ever seen. Tonight was a Voodoo Fire, and we were to be present"...
"The path climbed upward amongst the jagged hills. Below us lay the town and, far off, the sea, glittering in the moonlight. It was a warm, yet the pale rays of the moon cast a chill aura of malignant evil over the whole scene. We rode through a cemetery where the whitewashed tombstones flitted past like serried ranks of ghosts, then the dark shape of trees rose up again on either side, stretching their gnarled branches in our way. And all the while the hollow booming of the drums rang in our ears; now nearer, now further, rising and falling in subtle cadences. Often it seemed as if the sound were no more than half a mile away and then it faded into a distant throb. Strange...the nearer we approached, the fainter it became. But it never died completely away nor ever varied its rhythm. There were two distinct phases in the refrain. First the short, staccato: 'Tom-ti-ti-tom...luring and enticing; then the surging, heavy 'Boom-boom', threatening and compelling. The drums were calling, they drugged the will until all resistance died. I realized with impotent horror that it was impossible to turn back; the power of the drums was too great".

One can clearly see the importance of the Vodoun drum and the atmosphere it creates to literally draw in all who hear it and project their energy onto the Lwa. The drums are central to tapping into the human psyche and pulling out its primal nature to be utilized as a power source for contacting human and non-human entities. I also find it interesting that this first-hand account reads very much like that of Lovecraft's vision/nightmare, *"Nyarlathotep"* received by him in 1920, where the main character is compelled against his will *(as was Loederer)* into a vast swirling vortex of destruction and death, driven by the mad sound of beating drums and shrill terrifying flutes,

"My own column was sucked toward the open country, and presently felt a chill which was not of the hot Autumn; for as we stalked out of the dark moor, we beheld around us the hellish moon-glitter of evil snows. Trackless, inexplicable snow, swept asunder in one direction only, where lay a gulf all the blacker for its glittering walls. The column seemed very thin indeed as it plodded dreamily into the gulf...As if beckoned by those who had gone before, I half floated between the titanic snowdrifts, quivering and afraid, into sightless vortex of the unimaginable...And through this revolting graveyard of the universe the muffled, maddening beating of drums, and thin, monotonous whine of blasphemous flutes from inconceivable, unlighted chambers beyond Time; the detestable pounding and piping whereunto dance slowly, awkwardly and absurdly the gigantic, tenebrous ultimate gods – the blind, voiceless, mindless gargoyles whose soul is Nyarlathotep".
~ H.P. Lovecraft

There is a science to opening gateways; it is founded in three base principles; the Intent of the sorcerer, the use and release of static energy within angles and the vibration to imprint the sorcerer's Intent upon the Consensual Reality Matrix. With these tools, all is possible…

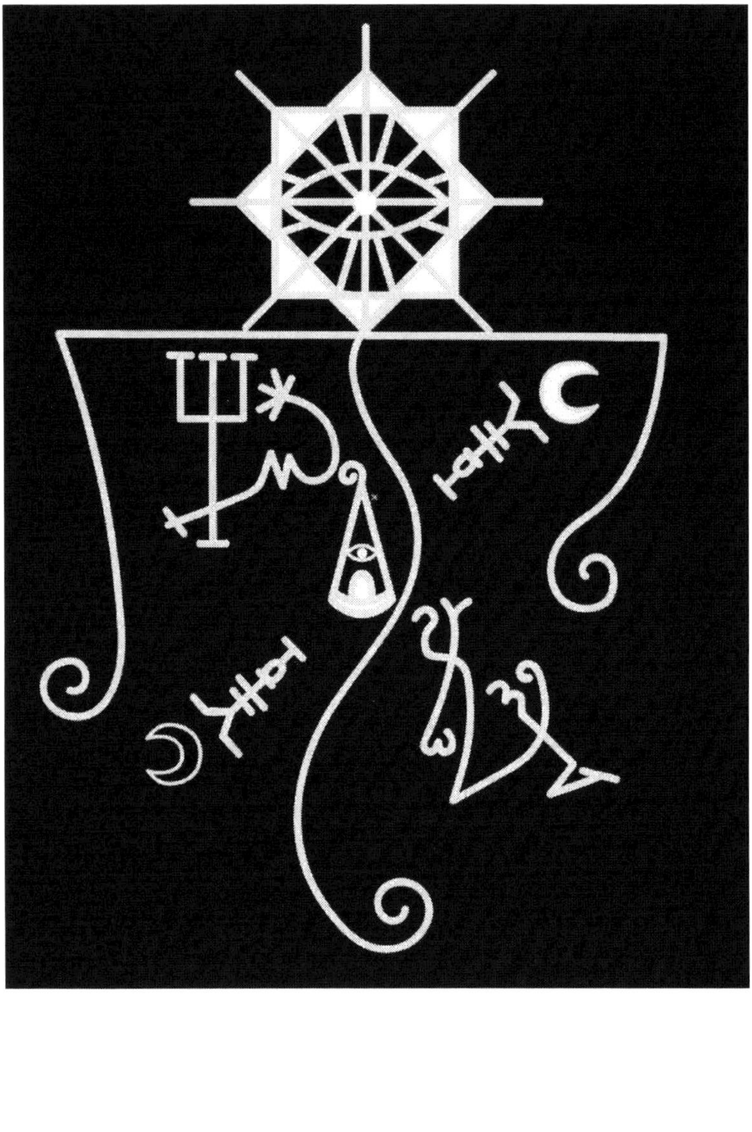

Final Word

When one thinks of me, they generally believe I am a Satanist in the most general sense of the term. I am not. I consider myself a *'Seeker of Truth Without Restraint'*. To seek *'Truth'*, one must not have boundaries confining them from that truth. One must not only explore one side of the proverbial coin, but both. For truth lies not on one side of the fence or the other, but is found on both sides equally. The *'Universe'*...it is my name for God. Many will immediately think I am speaking of the Judeo/Christian God, I am not. My concept of *'God'* is much larger than can be defined, it is a governing force outside of human understanding. On the Qabalistic Tree of Life, above Kether, there exist three more levels. These levels are *'Ain Soph Aur'*, *'Ain Soph'*, and *'Ain' (In ascending levels)*. Some Qabalistic texts only go up as far as. *'Ain Soph'*,

"You should know that the Creator, Ein Sof, is the cause of causes, one without a second, one that cannot be counted. Change and mutability, form and multiplicity, do not apply to it. The word 'One' is used metaphorically, since the number one stands on its own and is the beginning of all numbers. Every number is contained within it potentially, while it inheres in every number in actuality...The Creator is called one from this aspect: Ein Sof is present in all things in actuality, while all things are present in it potentially. It is the beginning and cause of everything. In this way oneness has been ascribed to the Creator; nothing can be added to this oneness or subtracted from it."
- Daniel C. Matt, *'The Essential Kabbalah'*

I don't generally *(if ever)* quote from Wikipedia, but this description fits well, so I will include it to assist in making my views clear,

> *"Ein Sof, or Ayn Sof (/eɪn sɒf/, Hebrew: אין סוף), in Kabbalah, is understood as God prior to his self-manifestation in the production of any spiritual realm, probably derived from Ibn Gabirol's term, "The Endless One" (she-en lo tiklah). Ein Sof may be translated as 'Unending', '(There is) no End', or 'Infinity'."*

My personal beliefs actually mirror that of Zurvanism in many ways. Zurvanism holds the belief that the deity known as Zurvan is *'One'* and *'Alone'*. Zurvan is something that is beyond *'Good'* and *'Evil'*, encompassing both aspects equally. Zurvan created duality in creating *'Ahura Mazda' (Being of Goodness)* and *'Angra Mainyu' (Being of Evilness)*. Both sprang from Zurvan and hold equal importance and value, while Zurvan is above both. This duality in unity can also be applied to the Judeo/Christian God when he states,

> *"I form the light, and create darkness: I make peace, and create evil: I the LORD do all these things."*
> - Isaiah 45:7

> *"The Lord hath made every thing for His own purpose, Yea, even the wicked for the day of evil"*
> - Proverbs 16:4

This belief is also represented in Taoism through the use of the Taijitu symbol, more commonly referred to as the Yin and Yang symbol.

Wuji
無極
No Extremity

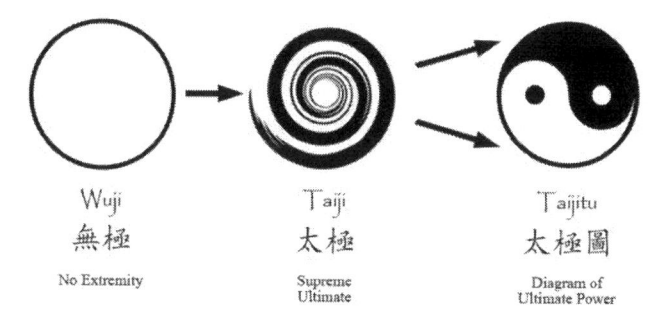

Taiji
太極
Supreme Ultimate

Taijitu
太極圖
Diagram of Ultimate Power

The Taijitu symbol represents *'Good and Evil'*, *'Light and Dark'*, *'Compassion and Hatred'* etc. encompassed into *'One'* intertangled form. This form consists as two separate forces working against each other *(but together)*, to cause *'Change'*, yet are encircled within one entity. One could see it as pistons moving in an engine to make it work, thus making the vehicle *'Move'*. Explosions in a car's cylinder move a piston, which through a long process, make the car move forward. Explosions are violent, two opposite forces combine and then reject each other immediately causing *'Change'*. What I am essentially and yet paradoxically speaking of, is *'Monistic Duality'*.

My belief as I said, is very similar to those just outlined. Like the Taijitu symbol, I believe there are two separate forces *(Chaos and Order)*, that work against each other, together to manifest change. However, in my belief one is not labeled *'Good'* or *'Evil'*. Both have equal importance and value. One is not stronger than the other, they are equivalent. However, too much *'Order'*, is a negative outcome. Order consists of *'Control'*, everything in its place, locked down and unable to create anything *'New'*. Order stifles creativity and expression at its base essence. That being said, too much *'Chaos'* is also a negative outcome. Chaos consists of the lack of *'Control'*.

Therefore, nothing can be organized to build effectively a permanency. One force needs the other to continue forward and any kind of progress be made, whether that be on a spiritual level or found within the material. One may ask why these forces must oppose or war against each other *(As an explosion)*. It is because if they were perfectly balanced, one even as the other as a calm sea, no change would occur. If change does not occur, experience does not occur, if experience does not occur, knowledge and growth does not occur. As I have written,

> *"These warring forces of Order and Chaos are evenly matched; One force rises up over aeons of time gaining supremacy, only to have the opposing force in turn rise up to push it back down, One force can never completely dominate the other. It is an eternal ebb and flow, so change can never cease in the Consensual Reality Matrix and experience never end, This cycle is eternal. It is as playing chess against oneself, only to stalemate match after match. The forces of Chaos and Order are equal. Though, calm between these two forces can never be known, now that the proverbial boat has begun to rock, they are set into perpetual motion. It is a game of tug of war that produces no victor."*
> - 'Thaumiel; The Dark Divided Ones'

As in Zurvanism, where *'Evil'* or *'Chaos'* are assigned to Angra Mainyu, and *'Good'* or *'Order'* is assigned to Ahura Mazda, so too do I believe spiritual entities in general are polarized to either one force or the other. As an example, there is Satan/Lucifer, Kali Ma, Set, etc. polarized to Chaos. Then on the other side of the coin there is Yehwey, Jesus Christ, Mithra, etc. polarized to Order. My belief also holds that people are also polarized to one force or the other. This is not a conscious choice, they are born with this polarization embedded within them, branded upon their very soul. I have aided many from both sides find their spiritual path, their true place. There are some that are born into a Christian family and are pulled towards the LHP. While there are others that the opposite has occurred. I have helped both gravitate towards their true polarization. Many have considered me *'Evil'* because of my polarization toward the LHP. I do not see myself as being malevolent, as I help people in general. I find great joy in assisting people with their daily problems, whether it be in matters of love, career or else. How can I be *'Evil'* while I am giving people peace of heart and mind ? It is all perspective in the end. And whether you are on one side of the fence or the other, both sides are equally needed and valid in their existence and purpose…

Et Facti Deo,
~ S. Ben Qayin

~ S. Ben Qayin ~

I have researched and practiced various forms of magic throughout my lengthy course of esoteric study, working in many areas of Ceremonial Magic. However, I discovered early on that magic was a thread that was woven through all things, and so was drawn to more personalized Chaos Magic from a young age. I hold the belief that magic is not *'magical'*, that it does not *'just happen'*, nor is it *'miraculous'*, I see it as a scientific system based on a process that we have yet to fully understand scientifically. This is based on my concept that humans do not fully realize the base structure of their reality in which they are currently residing, and that they have yet to understand all the rules of the *'Consensual Reality Matrix'*, and therefore do not entirely understand or utilize their personal energy and influence within it. I view magic as the manipulation of personal energy to restructure or influence the *'Consensual Reality Matrix'* to conform to the Intent of the magician. As with all energy, I believe magic can be harnessed and directed, spirits and entities can be contacted, and change can be made manifest within *'The Personal Reality Grid'* of the magician. I can assist you to unlock this hidden potential.

As the previous Head of the Inner Order of the Voltec, I have had years of training in shifting my perception of reality, and thus am able to successfully manipulate the *'Structure'*. The Order of the Voltec were an offshoot from The Temple of Set, which of course is an offshoot from LaVey's Church of Satan.

Chaos magic or *'Fringe Magic'* as I refer to it, is not new. It is simply a category or term created to encompass scientific magic or magic that deals with dimensions, non-human intelligences and work that questions the basis of reality, and how to manipulate it. This can be classified as experimental magic, teetering on the edge of the abyss of creation. Of course, Fringe Magic does encompass such literary works from authors and magicians who have ventured forth into the empty spaces, such as H.P. Lovecraft, Carlos Castaneda, Pete Carroll, Frank G. Ripel, Michael Bertiaux, Kenneth Grant and others who have been to the edge of creation and reality, and returned to write of it. They have masterfully transformed into words, experiences and concepts that are seemingly indescribable to those who have not walked the *'Spaces In-Between'* themselves, who have not known the *'Twilight of Being and Reality'*.

I Have Written:

"Volubilis Ex Chaosium"

"The Book Of Smokeless Fire"

"Harab Serapel; The Ravens Of The Burning God"

"The Black Book Of Azathoth"

"Thaumiel; The Dark Divided Ones"

"The Book Of Smokeless Fire II; Into The Crucible"

"S. Ben Qayin; The Collected Writings"

Contact Me Here:

Website: www.SBenQayin.com

Email: S.BenQayin@ymail.com

FaceBook: S Ben Qayin

Printed in Great Britain
by Amazon